00

01

Some Unique
Yorkshire Towns

Pontefract, Butter Market & St. Giles Church

Some Unique
YORKSHIRE TOWNS

Arnold N. Patchett

The Pentland Press
Edinburgh – Cambridge – Durham – USA

© Arnold N. Patchett, 1997

First published in 1997 by
The Pentland Press Ltd
1 Hutton Close,
South Church
Bishop Auckland
Durham

ISBN 1–85821-499-8

Typeset by Carnegie Publishing, 18 Maynard St, Preston
Printed and bound by Antony Rowe Ltd, Chippenham

ACKNOWLEDGEMENTS

On my travels there have been many men and women who have been only too pleased to help me and impart highlights of local history, unfortunately I never had the pleasure of knowing their names.

However, there are a number of people who have gone out of their way to help me in one way or another:

Mrs. M.E. Griffiths of Sedbergh School Library.

Mr. Michael Holdsworth of Pontefract and District Archaeological Society.

Dr. Arnold Kellett of Knaresborough.

The late Paul Buckingham who spent much of his life in Halifax.

I am also indebted to the late Frederic Riley for some of his writings in connection with past aspects of Settle.

A.N.P.

CONTENTS

ILLUSTRATIONS

Some Unique Yorkshire Towns

Photographs are taken from the author's own private collection.
Sketches are by Ruth Patchett.

INTRODUCTION

Sixteenth century Yorkshire was largely governed by its three separate Ridings, but this did not prevent the sense of community amongst Yorkshiremen, especially the county gentry. The peculiarities of speech and indeed, character, which distinguished Yorkshire folk has always been evident to outsiders.

In 1549 a learned gentleman of letters, Wm. Thomas, said: "Between the Florentine and Venetian is great diversitee in speeche, as with and as between a Londoner and a Yorkshireman."

The considered opinion of Edwin Sandys, Archbishop of York (1577–88): "A more stiff-necked, wilful or obstinate people did I ever know or hear of."

Nevertheless, a Yorkshire Farmer who corresponded with the Board of Agriculture's West Riding reporters in 1790 said:

"Ride a horse with a slack bridle and he will stumble less: he will depend on his own efforts. So it is with the lower order of mankind; the more bountiful we are, the more heedless and extravagant they are, I speak of the haughty and insolent. The aged and helpless will, I trust, ever meet with tenderness and compassionate assistance from their fellow creatures."

That Yorkshire Farmer's heart was obviously in the right place, in spite of Edwin Sandys' pronouncement!

By 1700, there were no less than 60 market towns in the county and by 1770 there were no less than 97 fairs throughout the year, each in a different place.

So let us have a look at some of these towns which I feel deserve very special attention. Rotherham, Halifax and Pontefract, whilst they do not figure prominently in popular tourists' ideas of places to visit, they have quite unique features in spite of and sometimes because of, industry and coal mining. Apart from Teesside little is known of Yarm, and perhaps Dent is a little 'off-beat'. Dent town is so described to differentiate it from Dentdale.

I have ignored the 'new' county boundaries which robbed Yorkshire in 1974 of large tracts of historic ground which it had looked after for centuries. Cities are not within the scope of this book.

A.N.P.

The Folly, Settle

SETTLE
CALDERDALE LIBRARIES

Once a snug little town unknown to the outside world, no castle, no king maker, no ancient church, no heroes of the Wars of the Roses – even Cromwell is said to have passed it by – yet . . .

Settle was granted a market as far back as 1248 – now held on Tuesday of each week – and was an important stopping place for stage coaches on the high road from York to Kendal. This highway still crosses the Ribble by means of the ancient bridge just west of the town centre. The bridge was deemed, even some 150 years ago, to need widening and the work was duly carried out at that time. Inspection at close quarters will reveal this on the north side which copes with great flood waters from time to time.

Overlooking the town is the now well known Castleberg, a huge precipitous limestone hill, described by Thomas Pennant, a famous antiquary, in 1773:

"At the foot of a monstrous limestone rock, called Castleberg, that threatens destruction, lies Settle, a small town in a litle dale, exactly resembling a shabby French town with a *place* in the middle. Numbers of coiners and filers lived about the place at this time entirely out of work, by reason of the salutory law respecting the weight of gold".

By contrast from evil doers, we learn that the Revd. Benjamin Waugh, who was born in Settle in 1839, was the founder of the Society for prevention of ill-treatment of children. Also Dr. George Birkbeck, born here in 1776, was the founder of Mechanics Institutes.

A very steep path leads one up to the summit of Castleberg, where there are convenient spots to sit, recover breath and admire the surroundings, which are many and varied. The whole layout of this quaint old town lies before us as well as the countryside to the south and the limestone areas to the north and west.

Some of the old buildings in the town have given way to new, but a number of ancient ones survive, including old courtyards and quaint nooks and corners. In the market place a row of shops and dwellings still stand with arched arcading rising from the roadway and a walk-way on top giving access to the uppermost floors. The whole is known as the Shambles. Opposite is a café, formerly an inn known as the Naked Man; a stone carving of the figure of a man over an outer door dated 1663 arouses much curiosity. Just off the market place is a beautiful house known as The Folly, built in 1675 as a gentleman's residence. From outward appearances, it looks superb, but may not have been completed as originally planned. In any case funds were not sufficient to enable the owner to live in keeping with the size and beauty of it. An antique shop now occupies a large part of it.

One has only to explore the streets and alleyways at the foot of Castleberg to find little gems of the past.

Almost inseparable from Settle is the village of Giggleswick with its famous school dating back to 1507, and ancient church of St. Alkelda. At the side of the now old road from Settle and Giggleswick to Kendal is a most extraordinary well, lying at the foot of a limestone cliff – the southern extremity of the Craven fault – it is known as the Ebbing and Flowing Well. A mile out of Settle, it consists of a rock trough usually full and overflowing, but from time to time the water level drops to within an inch or so of the bottom and then rises up again. There are two openings at the bottom of the trough and very occasionally a string of bubbles passes through the water from one opening to the other, this is known as the Silver Cord. It seems that some siphonic action takes place at certain times depending on the water supply which may vary according to weather conditions, though the latter do not always appear to account for the phenomenon. It is only feared that some over zealous person might interfere with the well in an attempt to discover its secrets, and find, to everyone's sorrow, that he has ruined this curiosity which so many visitors come to see. One can only hope that it will be a case of leaving well alone!

It is interesting to note that William Camden, the one time antiquary, produced his book *Britannia* in 1586. His remarks about the well:

"At the foot of a very high mountain at Giggleswick is the most noted spring in England for ebbing and flowing, sometimes thrice in an hour; and the water subsides three quarters of a yard at the reflux, though thirty miles from the sea".

Settle and Giggleswick achieved great publicity in the spring of 1927 when the total eclipse of the sun took place. The area was considered to be one of the best sites from which to view it, and crowds of sightseers covered the hillsides. A slow moving cloud obscured the early morning sun and gave rise to some anxiety, but in the nick of time the cloud passed away and the expectant crowd cheered loudly as they saw the eclipse from start to finish. Many came from afar by train. One particular train which included parties of enthusiasts was held up in a tunnel on the way to Settle; when it arrived at Settle station the eclipse was over. Passengers descended on to the platform and dumped their cameras, telescopes and other equipment in indignation!

A great event for Settle was the building of the Settle-Carlisle railway line with its embankments, tunnels, viaducts and countless bridges. What is more, the railway station at Settle was built only a hundred yards or so from the main street. The Thames-Clyde and Thames-Forth expresses passed over the highway between the market place and the old bridge over the Ribble – a great sight in those days. In recent years the line was, of course, threatened with closure due to high cost of maintenance coupled with declining numbers of passengers. However, the formation of Friends of the Settle-Carlisle Railway has met with some success and at present the line has been reprieved and more passengers are enjoying this unique scenic route, with its wonderful mountain views and the crossing of the now famous Ribblehead Viaduct, on the way to Appleby and Carlisle. At Appleby the late Bishop of Wakefield, Rt. Revd. Eric Treacy, a railway enthusiast, has left his mark in the form of a plaque bearing his name which is fixed to the wall on the north-bound platform.

Back in Settle we are spoiled for choice – there are so many natural wonders. A half-hour's walk from Upper Settle takes us to Scaleberg Foss. At the first road junction at the top of the first hill, the right hand lane leads to the Foss which is found in a woodland setting. One is immediately intrigued with the course of the water which cascades some forty feet over a point where the Craven Fault makes an abrupt and oblique bend.

A footpath starts at the above mentioned road junction and takes us to Attermire Scar and Victoria Cave. Attermire Scar on a sunny day is almost dazzling in its whiteness. The cave is quite remarkable and now has an enormous entrance. Arrow heads, relics of Neolithic man, Roman coins, and animal bones of countless ages past have been found here as a result of excavations at different levels of the floors. It is wide open to the public and the views from the entrance are superb. More caves of reasonable access can be reached on and around Giggleswick Scar, high above the Ebbing and Flowing Well. On top of the scar, a path leads to the tiny village of Feizor and on the way is a remarkable relic of ages past – a Celtic Wall over twenty yards long and over five feet high. Here again are superb views, notably of Penyghent and the flat topped Ingleborough, and to the south, Pendle Hill, all inviting the fell-walker to make haste to scale them.

Stackhouse Lane, not far past the old bridge on the right, leads to Knight Stainforth with its lovely old hall, still with a few windows walled up to avoid the one time window tax. Down the steep lane from here is a gem of a pack-horse bridge with its beautiful single arch spanning the Ribble. Downstream is the famous Stainforth Foss whose waters plunge headlong into a very deep pool. Over the pack-horse bridge is another steep lane which leads to the main road and Stainforth village with its stepping stones over Cowside beck. Across the beck a lane leads up to yet another waterfall. At the top of the hill on the left is a footway leading down to Catterick Foss which is situated in a deep limestone cleft. There are two falls, the higher and the lower are quite different in character, but both are in well wooded surroundings. Catterick Foss is thought to be the most romantic in the Craven district and has impressed many visitors over the years, including one Henry Lea Twistleton, a man with a poetic frame of mind. He was born in nearby Winskill hamlet in 1847 and subsequently emigrated to New Zealand where he wrote the following:

> The budding ash perchance is bending
> Its bows above the rocky rift;
> Where, mountain born, the beck descending,
> Is white as winter's gleaming drift;

While I, self-exiled, far away,
Sit dreaming of a bygone day.

How oft when summer days are ending,
And eve's wide shadows strewed the land,
I sought the Foss in gloom descending;
While wondrous as a fairy wand,
Its voice, in stillness, to my ear
Brought music of another sphere.

From this far land I send my greeting
To thee, fair grove! to thee, bright fall!
Year after year, your charms repeating,
To hearts of weary workers call
And bid them seek, by wood and stream
The tender thought and soothing dream.

Settle's natural wonders can be seen in a different light if one visits the Falconry near the west end of the by-pass. There are a great many adult birds to be seen there, from Kestrels to the Andean Condor, the largest. In addition to it being a tourist attraction, the Falconry encourages school visits and takes conservation of birds very seriously. To make a visit can be an education – you are invited to put a large thick glove on your left hand; the falcon or other bird of prey is called from its perch some twenty or thirty yards away. It immediately takes off and swoops on to your gloved hand which you hold aloft, and is fed. An eagle will be released – it soars away and disappears over the trees, but soon it is seen again circling round, its 'eagle eye' looking for prey. As soon as it sees it, down the bird swoops with split second timing – a fantastic example of co-ordination of the eye and muscular action. In 'captivity', the bird seems to know it is going to get its food regularly, whilst in the wild, it can be a more uncertain affair.

For a town enabling so many wonders to be experienced within a comparatively short distance, Settle must surely take a pride of place. Only a few miles away are the Norber boulders, enormous blocks of stone alien to the area are strewn at random over many acres of limestone based land, presumably having been brought down and deposited when melting took place towards the end of the Ice Age.

As a centre for the geologist, speleologist, naturalist and nature lover the little town of Settle must be very hard to beat.

SKIPTON

How did it get its name?

In the Domesday Book, it is described as Sceptone. The Saxon word for sheep is Sceap, so the vast area of sheep rearing centred on this town would surely be the origin of the name.

From whatever direction this historic town is approached, a road sign tells us that Skipton is the Gateway to the Dales. At first one feels that this is disputable, but on second thoughts, it must be admitted that the statement is correct, though perhaps lower Airedale does not exactly fit the popular conception of 'The Dales'. Skipton is, of course, in Airedale and placed in the widest part of the Aire Gap through which the river flows some distance from the town. In fact it is separated by the Leeds and Liverpool Canal and also the railway. The Aire Gap is, therefore, no mere narrow defile in the chain of lofty hills from the Scottish border to Edale in Derbyshire, it is probably almost a mile wide. The old route from places such as Leeds and Bradford came this way to reach central and northern Lancashire. Then followed the eighteenth century canal and the nineteenth century railway. Some 1800 years before that, the Romans lost no time in finding the Aire Gap and constructed through it one of their famous roads from York to Ribchester. They established a camp at Elslack, not far from the Gap, but found it difficult to defend the wide opening between the hills.

Five roads lead in and out of Skipton. The first is over the 'saddle' to Linton, Threshfield, Grassington and beyond to Amerdale, Langstrathdale and into Wensleydale. The second is the road to the west which leads to Malhamdale. The third takes us to the lower reaches of Wharfedale via Bolton Priory and Ilkley. The fourth takes us to Ribblesdale and Lancashire.

Let us take the fifth and enter Skipton from industrial West Yorkshire. A pleasant way is to leave the Aire Valley trunk road at Kildwick, pass over the very ancient bridge and follow what was once the old turnpike road into Skipton, over the canal bridge and into the High Street of which only one third is highway. One finds it hard to believe that Skipton has a double by-pass, one to the north and one to the south, as the traffic through the town is endless. Apart from through traffic, a great many come to go shopping as well as to enjoy the town's many attractions.

The first impression as one enters the High Street is the church, standing, as it were, guardian of the broad highway at the very top. Before we proceed further, however, it is well to step aside and go up Sheep Street and have a look at the old Town Hall. Access to it is gained by means of 13 steps with hand rails at each side. It is rather severe looking and double fronted, but the doorway boasts a stone pediment, popular in Georgian times. The building once housed the West Riding Quarter Sessions and men and women often entered there with their hearts in their boots, but when it was serving as a Town Hall, things were a little more

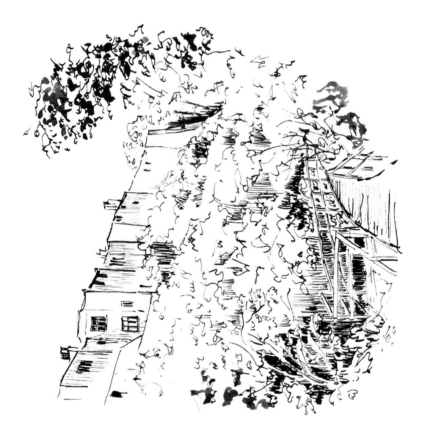

Skipton Castle and its wooded ramparts

homely. The old order changeth . . . for having been a gift shop of late, it is now divided into two parts upstairs. One large room is the Information Centre and the other is a meeting room, the attractively built information centre in the new Victoria and Albert area having been found too small. On each side of the entrance steps are said to be the remains of the town stocks, but to the untrained eye they are not easy to spot. At just below street level are shops. Above the Tea Shop, a plaque bears the legend:

THIS BUILDING WAS FORMERLY
THE TOWN HALL OR TOLL-BOOTH.
BENEATH ARE THE PRISON CELLS
WHERE FELONS WERE INCARCERATED
AND BRANDED. AT EACH SIDE OF THE
STEPS ARE THE REMAINS OF THE
TOWN STOCKS

This was the home of the Skipton
Mechanics Institute by whom this
tablet has been erected

The present Town Hall is, of course, near to the top of the High Street and contains an interesting museum.

The old Town Hall is one of several buildings which divide the lower part of the High Street into two – the narrow street thus formed is known as Sheep Street, at the top of which market days are held. Skipton has had its Charter for centuries. Originally it held a market on Saturdays and also two fairs, St Martin on 11th November and St John on 25th January, as well as one on the eve of Palm Sunday, Whit Monday and St. Luke's Day, 18th October. As these were not enough a Charter was obtained by George, 3rd Earl of Cumberland, for a fair to be held every second Wednesday from Easter to Christmas! George was a great favourite of Queen Elizabeth I and he commanded the *Bonaventure* against the Spanish Armada. To summarise the matter of market days, we now find them in Skipton every Monday, Wednesday, Friday and Saturday.

The livestock market was for many years held behind the present Town Hall, but two moves since then find it at the junction of the Gargrave road and the by-pass. The large area behind the Town Hall is, of course, the main car park and if this is not enough, there are two others just round the corner on the Gargrave road.

On the four days mentioned, the stalls occupy both sides of the cobbled High Street. They have their backs to the highway so as to face customers on the crowded side walks. On the left hand side of the street going up are numerous little side streets and alleyways. One of these in particular leads to a fascinating development. There is Albert Street, Victoria Street and a Square in which sturdy Doric columns support the upper portions of the shops, and afford shelter from the rain for shop window gazers and customers alike. All the buildings are more or less re-constructed with sand blasted old stone, with a delightful result. From here it is convenient to approach the marina where canal cruises can be taken and boats hired. Ducks abound and form a lively foreground for artists and photographers. The parish church tower forms a fitting background.

Back in the High Street, we cross over and enter Craven Court. This is another modern development and consists of a most attractive shopping area and places to refresh oneself in pleasant surroundings.

As we approach the church, we pass the spacious Black Horse hostelry and on the other side of the street is the very ancient Red Lion. Both have great character. Skipton Church stands serenely several feet above the roadway, and one can sit on one of the seats in the churchyard facing down the High Street and decide what one is going to do next – there are so many choices – or simply meditate and watch the world go by. Behind are the ancient stones drenched in history, and in front is the very essence of present day life: endless streams of traffic, shoppers, tourists, business men and women, the oddly dressed and the smartly dressed, farmers, old and young, mothers and their children, all attracted in their different ways by the magnetism of this unique town.

Inside the ancient stones of the church, we are at once struck with a sense of awe and peace contrasting strongly with the scene of hustle and bustle we have just left. One is, however, rarely alone as there is usually someone who will be pleased to point out the special features of which there are many. The present church was founded about 1300 by the canons of Bolton Priory. One of the most striking parts is the beautiful sedilia on the south wall; it has four seats for the use of the clergy during mass – the easterly one was formerly a piscina for washing vessels after Holy Communion. Above the sedilia is the Royal Coat of Arms of George III, dated 1798. It shows, in brilliant colour, the three lions of England, the lion of Scotland, the fleur de lys of France, the harp of Ireland and the arms of George, Elector of Hanover.

We always associate Lady Anne Clifford with Skipton among the numerous other places where she left her mark, in quite a different way from Mary, Queen of Scots. Lady Anne appears to have been a very busy woman indeed and we wonder when she had time to sleep anywhere! Following damage done during the Civil War, she, at her own expense saw that numerous renewals and repairs were done, including reglazing a number of windows. We cannot fail to notice that four windows bear her initials in colour, two with 'A P' and two with just 'P'(Pembroke) A.D.1665. Of course, a number of her forbears were buried here as will be seen by the elaborate tombs. Alas, the great lady was buried at Appleby, the home of her mother, though she was born in Skipton.

A curious feature of the church is the north door, and the other adjacent openings attract our attention. The early fourteenth century doorway was discovered in 1909 when a passageway was being made to the new vestry. During the construction of the passageway, a small piece of brown paper was found bearing the words: 'Thys was playsed in thys dore when it was bilt up in the year 1777'. The reason for the existence of the adjacent openings is not clear.

Whilst there is no memorial tablet in the church, or indeed a board giving names of the valiant local men who fell in the 1939/45 war, their names are carved on the front pew of the side chapel at the head of the south chancel aisle.

It is interesting to learn that the first known vicar of Skipton was one Nicholas of Fangfosse, 1267. Fangfoss? A village between Stamford Bridge and Pocklington. The Patrons of the church were the Prior and Canons of Bolton Priory until the Dissolution, and since 1542 the Patrons have been the Dean and Chapter of Christchurch Cathedral, Oxford. As you will see on the east wall of the chancel, this is perpetuated with the shields showing the Cross of Bolton Priory and the Arms of Christchurch, Oxford.

Tearing ourselves away from Holy Trinity church, we are immediately confronted with the original gatehouse of the castle. Straightaway we see the handiwork of Lady Anne again; it was she who had the parapet added embodying the Clifford motto 'Henceforth' or, as it is carved in stone, 'Desormais'. This was in honour of her father, George. One has only to ascend the short flight of steps to enter the castle itself and shortly enter the famous Conduit Court, built by Lady Anne's great great Grandfather, the Shepherd Lord. Here a little quotation of Wordsworth will not be amiss:

> Both roses flourish, Red and White
> In love and sisterly delight
> The two that were at strife are blended
> And all old troubles now are ended.

And so the Shepherd Lord returned from exile, now that revenge for his father's bloody deeds at Wakefield was no longer sought.

Here again, much restoration was done by Lady Anne; little did she think that some 300 years later the yew tree she planted would be the admiration of countless visitors, or did she? She was certainly a far-seeing woman. One of the drain water heads bears her initials 'A P' and is still in good condition. The tree was planted to celebrate the end of the Civil War in 1658. Like Pontefract castle, Skipton survived three separate attacks from the Parliamentarians but in the end surrendered with honour. In that year it was occupied by the Royalists again, but this caused parliament to order the place to be 'slighted'. However Lady Anne sought permission to repair the damage ten years later and, what is more, obtained it! Hence the motto on the gate house.

And so, we have a complete castle, well floored with a sound roof over our heads. As well as the Conduit Court, we can explore upstairs and downstairs and find the most attractive rooms as well as a dungeon.

Skipton Castle

The entrance to the castle in fact is only slightly raised from the High Street, but one is astounded with the view from the windows on the top floor. One can see for miles around from the west, north and east, and on looking down one realizes that it would be very difficult if not impossible to make an assault from those angles, because the castle's foundations are built on the edge of a sheer cliff some 260 feet from the waterway below. This is now the canal which served a nearby quarry and took stone to the Leeds and Liverpool canal. To reach the foot of the cliff there are two ways. The more interesting is to cross the main road from the steps to the west of the churchyard, then descend more stone steps which lead to the canal tow-path, go under the road bridge and eventually find oneself on a raised footpath. On one side of this is the canal and beetling cliffs; on the other is a swift flowing rivulet – a feeder of the nearby corn mill. The footpath leads onwards and upwards passing attractive properties – then one can lean on the wooden rail and see how impregnable the castle must have been from this angle. Only the entrance side needed serious defence. Time proved this.

Over the door to the Tudor Entrance is the following legend:

THIS SKIPTON CASTLE WAS REPAIRED
BY THE LADY ANNE CLIFFORD, COVNTESSE
DOWAGER OF PEMBROOKEE, DORSETT, AND
MONTGOMERY, BARONESSE CLIFFORD, WEST
MERLAND, AND VESEIE, LADY OF THE HONOR

OF SKIPTON IN CRAVEN, AND HIGH SHERIFF
ESSE BY INHERITANCE OF THE COVNTIE
OF WESTMORELAND, IN THE YEARES 1657
AND 1658, AFTER THE MAINE PART OF ITT HAD
LAYNE RVINOVS EVER SINCE DECEMBER 16
48, AND THE JANVARY FOLLOWINGE, WHEN
ITT WAS THEN PVLLD DOWNE AND DEMOL
ISHT, ALLMOST TO THE FOVNDACON, BY THE
COMMAND OF THE PARLIAMENT, THEN,
SITTINGE ATT WESTMINSTER, BECAVSE
ITT HAD BIN A GARRISON IN THE THEN
CIVILL WARRES IN ENGLAND. ISA.CHAP.
58. VER.12. GODS NAME BE PRAISED.

Can one say more?

The far eastern wing is not open to the public but the major part, which is open every day, will surely satisfy most, if not all of us. There are two other places the visitor should not miss before he leaves the castle; the first is the shell room constructed in the early seventeenth century – this is within the bounds of the Gateway towers. The other is the shell of the thirteenth century chapel of St. John the Evangelist which can be seen in the grounds of the castle to the left after passing through the Gatehouse.

The Parsonage, Haworth

HAWORTH

A visitor from abroad might well conjure up a vision of dark satanic mills set in a semi-remote valley in industrial Yorkshire. Rather should he think of a bleak windswept little town with a background of heather clad moors and a parsonage from which emanated stories which have captivated countless readers the world over. When one arrives in Haworth, it is not the general surroundings one has come to see first, but the now famous parsonage and church. What one soon learns is that the three Brontë girls did not spend their lives cooped up in the parsonage. Obviously it had some influence on them, but they travelled around and were inspired by what they saw and felt both near at hand and afar.

In the heart of Brontë country, then, stands the town of Haworth, its feet firmly planted on the floor of the steep-sided valley of a tributary of the river Worth. The town holds its head on a slightly sloping plateau a few hundred feet above. There one finds the famous parsonage, church, the Black Bull, ancient stocks, Post Office, Apothecary and unique shops and, of course, an Information Centre. The body of the town might well be described as a very long and very steep street, not quite straight and lacking in pavements for some part of it. To some, it appears hard and even forbidding – well, perhaps it does, especially on a cloudy, rainy day, but surely that's part of its character which often endears itself to the visitor who sees through the mere exterior. It is almost traffic free, so one can take a leisurely stroll up or down without having to dodge the ubiquitous motor car. Any traffic of that description is on an 'Access only' basis. At the lower end the street widens and a modern road, Rawdon Road, starts and takes travellers to the top of the hill where there is ample space and parking.

There is something rather special about the rugged quaintness of this unique street, which instead of nestling in the valley on the banks of the little river, climbs up the hillside with its odd buildings comprising shops, houses, inns, cafés. Not one of the scores of them, surely, is like its neighbours. It is inevitable that many of the establishments in and around that famous street use the name Brontë to describe their café, tea room or the goods they sell. To the literary bent, Haworth seems to have become a convenient stopping place between Stratford on Avon and the English Lake District – not surprising!

We are now at the top of the street and in our haste to visit the parsonage which, of course, is a 'must', we reluctantly pass the church door with its welcome sign and go up the narrow street to enter the parsonage garden. The parsonage itself is a large Georgian house occupied by Revd. Patrick Brontë for 41 years. It was later extended to the north in 1878 by Revd. Brontë's successor, Revd. John Wade.

Although the three sisters lived the greater part of their lives in Haworth, it must be recorded that they, along with their brother, Branwell, were born at

Thornton, Bradford, but shortly after baby Anne was born in 1820, their father became incumbent of Haworth, still in the parish of Bradford at that time.

Let us enter the church by the little north door and we are at once struck with the beauty of the place which only dates from the late nineteenth century. The church of Patrick Brontë's day was dismantled in 1879 amidst a certain amount of opposition, but it was generally agreed that the interior of the old building was ugly and indeed, inconvenient, with a central row of pillars and a three-decker pulpit along one wall making seeing and hearing the preacher very difficult. If one is curious as to how the outside looked before demolition, one has only to go to the south porch and look at the framed painting which hangs there.

The tourist magnet is the Brontë Chapel dedicated by the Bishop of Bradford in July 1964 and approached from the south aisle. Near the entrance to the chapel is a show case containing fascinating documents, including the copy marriage certificate of Charlotte Brontë to Revd. Arthur Bell Nicholls, and a seventeenth century bible used by Patrick Brontë.

Under the east window is a most attractive alabaster relief Reredos based on Leonardo da Vinci's 'Last Supper'. It is often illuminated, to great effect.

Down the church steps we go. On our left are the old stocks. On our right is the Black Bull frequented by Branwell. Adjacent to one of the fireplaces is a bell-pull said to have been used all too frequently by him to order more victuals. Near the door outside is a plaque stating that Branwell was secretary of The Three Graces Lodge of Freemasons. Alas, not for as long as he might have done. The masons held their meetings at this inn.

Brontë Country stretches far and wide. The three girls certainly got around: Scarborough to Cumberland and Kirkby Lonsdale, Nidderdale to the Peak District of Derbyshire, Bradford and the Spen Valley, London and Brussels. We must, however, confine ourselves to fairly immediate surroundings, so let us first follow the footsteps of Emily.

> For the moors! For the moors where the short grass
> Like velvet beneath us should be!
> For the moors! For the moors where each high pass
> Rose sunny against the clear sky
>
> For the moors, where the linnet was trilling
> Its song on the old granite stone
> Where the lark and wild skylark was filling
> Every breast with delight like its own!
>
> What language can utter the feeling
> Which rose when in exile afar,
> On the brow of a lonely hill kneeling
> I saw the brown heath growing there?
>
> Well – well; the sad minutes are moving,

Though loaded with trouble and pain;
And some time the loved and the loving
Shall meet on the mountains again.

E.J.B.

So, we make our way to those moors which certainly had a great influence on Emily. The first mile or so can be conveniently made by car along the west road which leads to what is known as Penistone Country Park in which there are several spaces for parking a motor car. From here it is only a one and a half mile walk. There are three approaches to Brontë Bridge and waterfall and also to the clump of rocks in which one is likened to a chair. The first and lower approach is along a lane which eventually peters out into a track and then a footpath. The second is along a footpath, signposted direct from the road, adjacent to the park. The third is by way of Harbour Lodge, approached also from the same road just where it dips down towards Oxenhope. The signpost guides one along a fairly straight farm road and just before reaching Harbour Lodge one turns right through the heather and bilberries to a steep descent at the side of the Brontë waterfall. At the foot of this is the Brontë Bridge which crosses the Sladen Beck in very romantic surroundings. In season, unfurling bracken and foxgloves abound and add colour to the sometimes sombre surroundings.

The original bridge, alas, is no more, but the huge squarish stone standing in the water is inscribed and tells us that the original bridge was washed away during a devastating flood in 1989 and that the Brontë Society rebuilt it in 1990. It is, of course, a footbridge consisting entirely of stone, almost identical with the original. Downstream from the bridge, the valley narrows and deepens and after a storm the flood waters passing under it are joined by the waters of the waterfall. Together they roar down the valley in glorious tumult – a romantic scene indeed and well worth the treck from Haworth. Judging by the number of visitors from the world over, there's no doubt that the place possesses some magic, just as it did for Emily Brontë.

Not far away is the Brontë Chair – not quite so popular – but once at the bridge, the great urge is to carry on to Top Withens which is a good mile up in the hills. The reason is, of course, the house is said to have inspired Emily to write *Wuthering Heights*, her famous novel. From the bridge one climbs a very steep and rocky slope to a signpost (in English and Japanese); we take the path to the left and follow the valley below us, gradually gaining height until the Pennine Way is reached and follow the now paved path to Top Withens – now roofless but cemented on top of the walls which for the most part stand almost exactly as they did in Emily's day. A more isolated spot, there can surely be few, is not easy to imagine, though a sycamore with two trunks stands to the windward wide and its boughs remain unbent against the relentless onslaught of westerly gales.

Do not be surprised to see smiling Japanese girls coaxing an old ewe to pose

Top Withens, Haworth

for them with the ruin as background. The sheep would be more than reluctant to do this for them if another visitor were sitting there eating his sandwiches. Let the visitor turn his head for a second and the sheep would think nothing of a snatch and grab!

On the wall of Top Withens is a large stone plaque bearing the following legend:

TOP WITHENS
THIS FARMHOUSE HAS BEEN ASSOCIATED WITH
"WUTHERING HEIGHTS"
THE EARNSHAW HOME IN EMILY BRONTË'S
NOVEL
THE BUILDINGS, EVEN WHEN COMPLETE, BORE
NO RESEMBLANCE TO THE HOUSE SHE
DESCRIBED,
BUT THE SITUATION MAY HAVE BEEN IN HER
MIND WHEN SHE WROTE OF THE MOORLAND
SETTING OF THE HEIGHTS

Brontë Society	This plaque has been placed here
1964	in response to many inquiries.

The Japanese visitors and indeed many others will take a photograph of the plaque and take the record of it to the other side of the world. Another example of the Brontë magic. How long the magic will last, none can tell, but so long as those ancient walls, there on that windswept hillside, stand up, visitors will come and say with pride that they have been and seen.

We should now return to Haworth, or Stanbury and motor to Wycoller, via the road to Colne. When we reach the entrance to Wycoller Country Park, we descend on foot to the once little known hamlet of Wycoller itself by means of a steep path at the side of the old coach road. As we descend, the most notable thing is the presence of Vaccary walls. These consist of upright stone slabs placed edge to edge, and date back to far beyond the time of the enclosure system. They were used when cattle were driven to gather at a given area. Unique.

In the hamlet itself the little river is spanned by several bridges, clapper and pack-horse. The charm of the latter lies in the fact that the arches are far from regular, and the paving on the bridge itself is U-shaped through the passage of so many pack-horses in the past, later by so many boots and shoes of villagers, and later still by many tourists. Motor traffic is barred except for residents and handicapped visitors. Adequate car parks are available on the Trawden Road and on the Haworth Road.

At the time of the Brontës, Wycoller was a busy little village of about 350 people, many of whom were connected with the textile industry. The Hall would be occupied then but with the coming of the industrial revolution, the population declined as the cottages which housed hand looms became vacant and indeed, derelict. A number have been demolished during the past few decades. The Hall also fell into ruin, but before that, Charlotte Brontë was known to have visited Wycoller and its Hall which has been recognised as the Ferndene Manor featured in *Jane Eyre*. Here again the Brontë fans come to explore the hamlet, especially the Hall, even though it is in ruins – cared for, nevertheless. Apart from the Brontë connection, Wycoller is a most attractive place. All the remaining dwellings have been attractively restored, along with the pack-horse bridge and the several clapper bridges crossing the babbling little river which passes the frontage of the Hall. Altogether, they are a mecca for both artists and photographers. The one-time barn at the top end of the hamlet has been restored and contains a large and fascinating collection of farm implements of the past and many remnants of the former textile industry.

Prior to the industrial revolution, Haworth like many more little towns, possessed the hardy folk who operated hand looms as well as farming, but the textile mills which arose around the foot of the town saw the end of the hand loom. After the Brontë period, Haworth became a busy textile town and with it had a railway of its own to Keighley, via Oakworth, and to Oxenhope where there is a good railway museum. Many of us know the T.V. story of the *Railway Children* with scenes at Oakworth station. Haworth, however, is the headquarters of the Worth Valley Railway Preservation Society. It is a shining example of the

Haworth Railway Station

devotion of its members; the booking hall at the station has retained its original aura and is in an excellent state of repair and decoration. There is a gift shop on the premises, and it is a wonderful place for a railway enthusiast to browse whilst waiting for a train, or even if he isn't. There is also a Ladies' Room which is entered from the platform. The paintwork everywhere is immaculate, and hanging baskets alternate with original gas lamps along the platform.

A whistle and a low rumble can be heard in the distance; up the valley comes a restored steam locomotive drawing several carriages, all genuine and restored; it comes to a stop with much ado. A scene of animation follows as passengers alight and some join the train for the last lap to Oxenhope. It can be a moving experience – a reminder of the one time great importance of the arrival of a train at a rural or semi-rural station. There is a footbridge at the southern end of the platform which gives direct access to the town head. On it you will often see amateur photographers with their cameras at the ready for the arrival of a train. Late morning is, perhaps, the best time to take a picture on a summer's day.

The Railway Yard, adjacent to the station, is open to the public and there are many locos of different types and sizes – from enormous steaming giants to the modest looking bankers. Some are waiting to be restored and perhaps one or two ready for action. Yet another rendezvous for the railway enthusiast!

In addition to daytime services at weekends from Keighley to Oxenhope and back, there are regular trains every day during the summer months. There are also special events throughout the year with Pullman and dining car carriages pulled by locos with famous names. The Worth Valley Railway is the only complete branch line in the country which is run privately.

So we say Goodbye to Haworth, bearing in mind that the Brontë associations extend to so many other places such as Oakwell Hall, Birstall, The Clergy Daughters School at Cowan Bridge, near Kirkby Lonsdale and Miss Patchett's school near Southowram, Halifax. Regrettably these are outside the scope of this little book.

HALIFAX

From Hell, Hull and Halifax, Good Lord Deliver me.

This was the highwayman's view. In the case of Halifax, it would be most likely the town's infamous gibbet which caused this well known phrase to be coined. As for romantic history, Halifax has this in good measure, and from the tourist's point of view, one has not to move far from Commercial Street to discover it. Almost the whole of the town is situated on an inclined plane from King Cross down to the river Hebble at the foot. As we start from the river in a westerly direction, rising all the while, we see the railway and mills which conjure up names such as Mackintosh and Patons and Baldwins (shades of toffee and the spinning of wool), long since moved elsewhere, alas. Let us not despair, however, because there are still active industries in their place.

Horton Street then, leads us up to the town centre, but on our right is the ancient parish church, black with ages of soot and grime, once serving one of the largest areas in the country. It is often locked and no wonder, in view of the priceless treasures it contains. To obtain the key it is necessary to visit the verger's house which is quite near. Once inside the church, one is immediately struck with the sheer beauty of the place. This is not a parish church which one might easily expect to find in an industrial town in West Yorkshire. It is thought that the first church was a Saxon one; even so, the first church on this site dates back to circa 1120 and was built by the monks of far away Cluniac Priory of Lewes in Sussex, to whom had been given the Halifax part of the huge Manor of Wakefield by the Second Earl of Warrenne about that time. Fragments of the Norman building can still be seen in the north wall and crypt. Finally, in the fifteenth century thanks to a bequest by the vicar, John King, and increased prosperity in the town, rebuilding on an extensive scale took place under the next vicar, Thomas Wilkinson, who also gave generously.

The visitor who is interested in architecture alone will find the place packed with features to appreciate and indeed, admire, especially the ten arcades from the west end of the nave to the east window, including the chancel and choir. The windows, of great variety, are of interest in themselves. To the Puritans, stained glass with its 'graven images' was not the thing, so that during the Commonwealth in the mid seventeenth century a number of plain glass windows were inserted, but the leads were arranged in a quite unique and striking pattern. It is thought that no other church has such Commonwealth glass arranged in such beautiful design. The great west window is a restoration of a Commonwealth window dating from 1657. The great east window, however, is noted for the brilliance of its colours, but was not inserted until the second half of the nineteenth century. On the north wall, most of which was the original south wall, are windows which date back to the Norman period. The rose window, high up on the south

The Elbow on the Magna Via on its way down to Halifax

wall, forms part of the memorial to the Rawson family who played a great part in the history of the town.

Jacobean pews abound and date from 1633. Each has a gate and the intricate carving on each and every one as well as on the pew ends gives one an idea of the great care and dedication of the men who did the work. The height, many years ago, was lowered by as much as two feet since they were first made.

Side chapels include the Chapel of Resurrection – now a memorial chapel of the 33rd. Duke of Wellington's Regiment. On the left proudly hang the colours of the regiment from 1854 – 79, Alma, Inkerman, Sebastopol, and in 1868 Abyssinia. The Duke's Regiment has always been associated with Halifax and a small regimental Headquarters still occupies part of the barracks established in 1873 in the town. At the Bankfield Museum, which is approached from North Bridge, a little way up the road to Queensbury, is a fascinating collection of all aspects of the regiment and its history. The building was once the home of Col. Edward Akroyd, a wealthy Halifax mill-owner. It is interesting to note that only twenty years after the Colonel spent some £20,000 on additions and alterations, the Halifax Corporation bought the mansion and parkland for a mere £6,000 in the latter half of the nineteenth century with the purpose of forming a museum.

Back in the church, the Holdsworth and the Rokeby Chapel, recently refurbished, are worthy of special note.

The basement was said to be a charnel house, but in 1626, vicar Robert Clay changed all that. He was a follower of Sir Thomas Bodley, who built and furnished the University Library at Oxford, and of his helpmate, Sir Henry Savile, Warden of Merton College. That period was a golden age for Halifax scholars and builders; it was then that a library was established in the basement, and must have been one of the finest church libraries in existence. It contained eight volumes which were printed prior to 1488 as well as the work of Henry Briggs (1560 – 1630) who was a Halifax scholar and Oxford professor. In one of the books presented by him there is a copy of his own logarithms of 30,000 numbers. Alas, the whole library of 270 volumes was, for safety reasons, transferred in 1966 to York University on permanent loan. The basement is situated under the chancel and can be entered from ground level as the church is built on ground which slopes from west to east. The doors are permanently locked and the entrance today is from behind the altar in the Duke of Wellington's chapel, and down a series of stone steps. Down there is the Choir room, various offices and the boiler house!

With our minds full of wonder and admiration for this ancient place of worship we are about to leave and make our way up to the famous Piece Hall when we are stopped in our tracks. There are two memorials, quite outstanding, near the south door. The first is to Bishop Ferrar who was martyred and burned at the stake in 1555. He had Halifax connections. The second, in colour, is the bust of Dr. Favour, who was vicar from 1593 to 1624, one of the most famous, if not the most famous of them all. He came from Southampton to Halifax some five years after the defeat of the Armada. He never minced his words and in the Registers he often added notes on the character of those he buried, e.g.

> 1597 Jan 24 William King of Skircoat
> "was a swearer, drinker . . .his last words
> were oaths and curses"
> 1600 Apl 15 Richard Learoyd 58 years
> "honest"

The bust forming his memorial is small but impressive and it is easy to imagine he would vex the ungodly so much so that there were two men in particular who vowed they would never enter his church again. However, they did, because soon afterwards they both fell ill and died and were buried by Dr. Favour!

At the south door is a gargoyle which represents the man who played the bagpipes on the gibbet before the condemned ones laid down their heads for the last time. More about the gibbet in a later chapter.

Which way did those Norman knights, monks, pilgrims and their followers come from Sandal Castle, Wakefield and the south to Halifax? Having reached what is now Hipperholme, they came up a very steep hill and over the brow of Beacon Hill and down very, very steeply, to where Clark Bridge now stands, then up a short distance to reach their Mecca. Later the route was used by pack-horses but as Daniel Defoe said in 1774 'the Hill which they go up to come out of the town towards Leeds and which the country people call Halifax Bank is so steep, so rugged and sometimes too, so slippery, to a town of so much business as this, 'tis exceedingly troublesome and dangerous'.

Let us tread on those ancient setts of stone paving from Hipperholme. First of all there is a steep and wide paved road down from the one-time Railway Station then a turn to the right to Norcliffe Lane. A short distance up the latter there is a sign which reads: DARK LANE – Hollow Way Ancient Monument, then a five-barred gate through which one immediately sees a well built pedestal bearing the words MAGNA VIA, on top of which is a metal plaque giving a short history of the trackway. Just after passing the entrance to Lower Place Farm, a gritty but wide path leads to a well paved way, about eight feet wide with high banks and trees on each side. It ascends steeply, but after a time becomes narrower as one reaches the top, after a good half mile when high walls appear on each side. Eventually it emerges into open bleak country and an old lane, Barraclough Lane. One is then almost on Beacon Hill, and if you carry straight on, on the left you will see a series of what are not unlike upright vaccary stones. Keeping to the right and leaving the lane, Halifax in its entirety as well as miles and miles of surrounding country appears before you. Soon the paving reappears and it is easy to follow. Here the once bare hillside has been planted with masses of attractive shrubs and rhododendron; then comes the 'Elbow', a wonderful example of road making technique. In dry weather in late spring, one can safely descend whilst admiring the colourful blooms, but in rainy weather it brings to mind Daniel Defoe's words 'so slippery'. Part of the way down one finds there is a footpath somewhat raised from the old track. Eventually one comes to a full stop on reaching the modern road from Halifax to Southowram. Cross this road obliquely and descend yet another very steep paved path through the woods until it emerges into a very wide paved road, closed to traffic, which leads right down to Clark Bridge; a stone's throw ahead stands the ancient church.

The route we have just traversed has its attractions, but one wonders why a more roundabout and much easier way was not taken. Or was the Roman bug for taking a bee-line still in the blood of those who, so painstakingly, planned and made the route? Be that as it may, there cannot be any other industrial town such as Halifax which possesses such a unique track. The MAGNA VIA.

The Piece Hall – A piece of what? It is not exactly a hall, either.

The Calder Valley and the Hebble Valley, with abundant supplies of soft water, and land suitable only for pastoral farming, the textile industry became a major part of life for some. A farmer could easily augment his income by installing a hand loom which he and his family could handle. The length of cloth would usually be about 30 yards and was known as a piece, and when it was dyed and finished it would be taken for sale to a Cloth Hall of which there were a few in West Yorkshire. The first in Halifax was known as far back as 1572, but with the great increase in demand for cloth during the next 200 years, Piece Halls were built in places such as Bradford and Huddersfield. Only Piece Hall Yard in Bradford and Cloth Hall Street in Huddersfield remain as reminders of that far off age, but in Halifax, the Piece Hall of Piece Halls was opened in 1779. There's a suggestion of Roman classical architecture about it; massive rustic piers support semi-circular arches on the ground floor, known as the Arcade level. Square jointed columns on the Rustic level and a continuous gallery of round Doric columns on the top floor or Colonnade complete the picture. At the corners is a staircase giving access to each floor. The entrances are in the middle of each of the four sides, but only the north entrance has the original studded oak doors. The other entrances are more modern but very attractive, especially the south gate which gives access from Horton Street.

Inside, the square covers about 10,000 square yards and is cobbled and paved for a good half of the area, but on the eastern side there is a well kept greensward with seats. The site has to be seen to be believed and is a credit to those who decided in 1972 to restore it to its former glory, although it was saved from destruction or complete ruin by only one Council vote. After more than a hundred years its use declined because of the power loom which came into use in the nineteenth century industrial revolution when enormous mills were built. Merchants no longer bought their cloth from the hand loom weaver and so the lovely old Piece Hall fell into decline in spite of public events being held there from time to time. Originally there were 315 rooms, each with a door and a window all facing the great quadrangle. Now there are at least 50 shops and an information centre. Bookshops, antique dealers, bric a brac, little art galleries and cafés fill the rooms in the various galleries.

The building, having been thoroughly cleaned, reveals a mellow creamy yellow sandstone. One famous view from the north-west corner of the arcades shows a slim church spire standing steadfast over the roof of the east Colonnade against a background of bleak hillside. It is not, of course, the parish church which has a tower, but that of a much later building, the nave and chancel of which have long since been demolished. Pity!

There is great animation on the cobbles on Fridays and Saturdays – a thriving market occupies a large portion of the spacious quadrangle. A few stalls display lengths of cloth, not whole pieces as formerly. Fruit and vegetables, drapery and bric a brac as well as children's toys abound.

As we leave the Piece Hall by the west gate with its domed bell-cote bearing a golden fleece and weather vane, we notice rather surprisingly that the outside of the building, apart from the gates, is almost entirely free from any form of decoration and is free from windows. This is true of three sides, but the north face with pilasters and arches in relief like those in the arcade, proves to be the exception. If we leave the Piece Hall by way of the north gate, we come to a very old shopping centre, Woolshops, now nicely modernised with an island of trees at the top where it joins Southgate. We turn left and find our way into Borough Market, one of the largest covered markets in the county. For a variety of goods at competitive prices, it must be hard to beat.

Just up from Southgate is Old Cook Yard, much reduced in size since the stage-coach days due to the encroachment of later buildings. However, the Old Cock Inn is still there and dates back to late sixteenth century. It contains, on the first floor, a magnificent banqueting hall with a stained glass window occupying the whole of one side of the room. There are no less than 20 lights and it is the third largest privately owned stained glass window in the country. The fireplace, with a masterpiece of wood carving which forms the surround, at once attracts one's attention. The date – 1591 – can be seen if one looks carefully. This room was occupied by 'The Loyal Georgians' on the first Wednesday in each month for something like 175 years.

One week before Captain Cook was killed in Hawaii, a group of Halifax citizens met on the steps of the Parish Church and agreed to form a Society. The reasons were:

"Whereas in consideration of the many afflictions which men are subject to, who are not in affluent circumstances to support themselves, and where or when it shall please Almighty God to afflict any of us, whose names and seals are hereunto subscribed and set, with Lameness, Sickness, Disease, Indisposition or old age, so as to render us incapable of working at our respective trade or business, we therefore, severally and mutually have proposed and agreed to the following Articles for our relief and support

Wainhouse Tower, Halifax

when we shall be so rendered incapable of earning our lively-hoods, thro' Lameness, Sickness, Indisposition, or old age, which we hope will render our condition more easy, comfortable, and satisfactory".
This was on February 3, 1779.

The Society still flourishes, but on account of re-organisation and change of ownership of the inn it meets elsewhere each month. Maybe in the not too distant future the Society will once more, meet in that famous old inn.

Our next port of call must surely be the Hall that Barry built.

If you approach it from Princess Street, a very attractive, but somewhat ornate tower, with clock, at once catches the eye. It is, of course, the tower of the Town Hall built in 'North Italian Cinquecento' style, but the architect, none other than Sir Charles Barry who designed the Houses of Parliament, obviously blended several styles into one. An early sketch by him submitted to Halifax Corporation cannot fail to suggest Big Ben's tower was still in his mind. However, the final which was accepted was a little different and as Sir Charles died as the actual work had just started, his son Edward who had assisted his father, took over. The tower is a masterpiece of carved decoration. Four angels, each well over six feet high, guard the spire; in between the angels are representations of the four major continents.

Inside the Hall, approached from Wesley Court is the great entrance hall leading to the Victoria Hall, open to the public on weekdays during office hours. Victoria Hall is typical of Barry's work, with balustrade and a highly decorated glazed roof. The whole was formally opened with long past (alas!) Victorian splendour, by the Prince of Wales on 4th. August 1863. Our first view of the tower from Princess Street reminds us that the Princess, unfortunately through illness, was unable to accompany the Prince on that memorable occasion. Celebrations of the event were held in the Piece Hall at which the Prince attended.

Leaving the Town Hall, we go up Crossley Street to a roundabout and on our right is a huge multi-storey car park. From here we go up Gibbet Street and quite soon, standing on a small paved square, the re-erected Gibbet shows itself. An imitation steel blade protrudes from a massive block of wood, down which it would fall on the neck of the committed. A brief history of the Gibbet is given on the spot from which it is noted that the first recorded execution took place as far back as 1288 when the unfortunate John Dalton met his fate. The last time it was used was 30th April 1680 when the punishment perhaps more than fit the crime.

Up Gibbet Street, we finally arrive at Queens Road and make for King Cross and a modernised road system with numerous traffic lights, about a mile from the town centre. Here we turn left and immediately note an enormous landmark – Wainhouse Tower. It stands on a rough piece of ground adjoining a burial ground on the brink of the Calder Valley. It thrusts itself quite splendidly into the sky – a Yorkshire version of an Italian Renaissance tower which seems to

Halifax Piece Hall

act as a foil to the surrounding flat topped hills, and brings the eye to rest on it in a turbulent landscape. The Octagon Tower, or Wainhouses's Folly as it has been often called, was begun in 1873 and took two years to complete by John Edward Wainhouse, a wealthy bachelor able to indulge a passion for building. It was first designed, without a pinnacle or corona, as a mill chimney with a staircase for the Washer Lane dyeworks which Wainhouse owned and let to a tenant. About that time a Smoke Abatement Act came into being and Wainhouse considered that any smoke from a chimney as tall as his would be blown well away before it had time to deposit the soot on the town. Other reasons for building a chimney of such a great height are sometimes put forward. A wealthy neighbour, Sir Henry Edwards, was not kindly disposed to Wainhouse, so that the latter, out of spite, built his chimney so high that its shadow cast itself from one end of Sir Henry's estate to the other!

Let us have a close look at the tower and its imposing entrance. It is 253 feet high and cost £15,000. The labour cannot have been cheap, because if you ascend even to the first balcony, the carved stonework at close quarters shows work of a rare craftsman or craftsmen; the attention to detail has to be seen to be believed. At the start, Wainhouse employed Isaac Booth, but when he discovered him to be Sir Henry's architect, he changed to a Mr Dugdale who did the fantastic corona. The staircase consists of 403 steps (92 more than the Monument near London bridge) and winds round and round between the brick chimney and the outer octagonal ashlar faced first class stone. At intervals slit windows as well as a nicely carved one give some light through the metal grilles. Birds used to nest on the window ledges until the grilles were fixed in recent times. Having climbed no less than 369 steps, one emerges onto the first parapet which enables the visitor to walk round protected by substantial balustrading surmounted with eight pinnacles and also columns which support the final parapet and later the corona. The final parapet is not considered safe for visitors and so the last 34 steps to reach it are closed to the general public, many of whom will be well satisfied and indeed thrilled with the views obtained in every direction. It is an easy climb for anyone of average soundness of wind and limb, as the steps are of such a size and shape that they can hardly be more easy on the feet.

The tower passed through many hands before a shilling fund was organised by the *Halifax Courier* and *Guardian* newspaper who presented it to the Halifax Corporation in 1912. The Calderdale Leisure services open the tower to the public on High Days and Holidays, including Father's Day, for a modest fee.

After all that, the Washer Lane Dyeworks closed down before the chimney was finished, but Wainhouse did not let that deter him from putting the final touches to his tower, so no smoke ever fouled that wonderful structure!

Apart from the views from the tower of the Calder Valley and Castle Hill, Almondbury (Huddersfield) and Blackstone Edge (Roman Road), the nearest object of interest lies far below. It is called Wainhouse Terrace. It is situated between the Burnley and the Rochdale Roads a short distance west of the traffic lights at King Cross, and consists of a beautifully built colonnade and terrace overlooking the Calder Valley with Wainhouse tower on the left. The terrace of houses which stood adjacent to the Burnley Road side were not considered worth retaining and in 1978 were demolished. However, the best architectural features, the colonnade, lower terrace and the turret in the middle, were retained. These unique remains call for continuing care and could become more of a tourist attraction than they are at present. They should not be missed by anyone who has only a modest interest in history and architecture.

Other tourist attractions in Halifax include the Industrial Museum immediately to the east of the Piece Hall. Museums are usually static, but the Industrial Museum actually works. You have the chance to see things working – the Spinning Jenny, steam engines (with live steam!) and looms. A great array of industries which sprang from this area are all there to experience – even to smell, touch and hear. The making of toffee is shown, and 'Cat's Eyes' shine in the darkness.

Noteworthy is 'Eureka' – the first museum in Britain for children. It is about the mysteries which lie behind, inside and underneath the surface of countless phenomena of this world of ours. The building covers a vast area, adjacent to a large car park and the Railway Station. It was opened in June 1992.

Halifax was not overlooked by Charles I (1600–1649). Apparently he was short of money and dared not ask Parliament for a grant in case he was asked how he intended to use it. He therefore approached the gentry up and down the country and offered a knighthood to men of some substance, and enriched himself by the fees that had to be paid by every new knight. Among others, he thought some of the men of Halifax would be fair game. If a knighthood were refused, a fine was imposed with the alternative of prison. Some of the men of this once enormous parish refused the knighthood and paid the fine: among these were Nathanial Waterhouse (Waterhouse Street) and Gregory Patchett who built his own house in Luddenden. This house is still standing and bears his initials over the door, viz 1634 G.G.P. The four is carved the wrong way round. It is an inn to-day and has been known for many years as The Lord Nelson. Luddenden is one of the quaintest, if not the quaintest of villages in the district. The position of the church and indeed the whole village is quite extraordinary, lying as it does not only at the side of its little river, but up the very steep sides of the surrounding hills. The High Street is very, very narrow with sharp angular turns which make even the speed merchant in his motor car make haste slowly.

As we go up the road to take our leave of Halifax, we are reminded of and indeed guided on our way with 'Cat's Eyes'. Not only do we see them in Halifax but throughout Britain and abroad for thousands of miles. They were, of course, invented by one Percy Shaw – a Halifax man.

PONTEFRACT

What do we know of Pontefract?

Pomfret Cakes and a race course immediately come to mind. Readers of Shakespeare will recall Act III Sc. 2 in *Richard III* in which Earl Rivers says about Pontefract Castle:

> 'O Pomfret, Pomfret! O thou bloody prison
> Fatal and ominous to noble peers!
> Within the guilty closure of thy walls
> Richard the Second here was hack'd to death . . .'

The race course goes back at least to the early eighteenth century and is now the longest circular course in Europe. Apart from the castle, built by the Normans, and liquorice which came from France and Spain at first, the town has a continental flavour and some fascinating features associated with Europe.

The approach from most directions can be very depressing with devastated mother earth and spoil heaps of gigantic proportions. Even the famous Prince of Wales colliery is not what it was. However, an interesting approach is from the Monkhill railway station, some distance from the town centre; a short walk brings you to a rocky knoll and above it stands the 'scant' remains of the once magnificent castle. Scant remains indeed, and a shadow of its former self maybe, but sufficient well cared for stones remain to build a fair sized village. The first stonework appears where the road from the station meets the main road, and is the base of the Swillington Tower named after Sir Robert Swillington who was the steward under the famous John of Gaunt, but even that has been cut in half on account of road widening. We cannot blame Cromwell for that!

As we turn to our left, we are surprised to see the ruins of a church, but on closer inspection we find that the present church of All Saints is built within the original. To enter, we pass through the time-worn and roofless arches of the old. Over the door of the 'new' church is a plaque which tells the story:

> ALL SAINTS
> This ancient parish church of Pontefract
> Present building 13th/14th. century
> Ruined in 1645 during Civil War. Tower and
> Transept restored 1831. New nave 1967
> Noted for double helix staircase sketched by Turner

The inner church with its north and south transepts, is beautifully kept, and its double helix stone staircase gives access to the tower – the latter is perhaps the outstanding feature of this extraordinary church with the richly carved tower parapet from which rises a rugged and crenellated octagonal lantern. The narrow

The Counting House Inn, Pontefract

staircase is entered through a low door at the corner of the nave and north transept outside the building. Indoors, a small doorway (another small doorway) in the north wall of the nave leads us up the stairway, and fifty-nine steps later a trap door is pushed over the top of the descending steps and one finds oneself in the bell chamber. Inside the surprisingly large chamber, there is a step ladder giving access to the bells and turret. To make the descent one pushes the trap door over the staircase which one has just ascended. The whole structure is supported in the middle by a single stone newel. A rare experience. The internal access has been restored comparatively recently, as a result of the new extensions during 1966/67. Formerly it was blocked up by rubble disposed of during the building of the transepts and foreshortened nave and chancel in 1832 and by the bellows of the organ erected in 1937. The entrance was plastered over!

As far as is known, there are only two such staircases in the British Isles. The other is at the church of St. Editha at Tamworth in the Midlands. It is thought that there is another in Normandy – again a connection with the continent.

Originally, the staircase at Pontefract led up to the top of the octagonal lantern some 80 feet from the ground. There were 99 steps in all. Maybe we can blame Cromwell as he partially destroyed the church!

In our haste to reach 'Bloody Pomfret', we must not miss The Booths; on the way up to the castle on the left hand side was a row of medieval shops, mainly butchers. There is only one cottage on the site today, but on its wall there is a plaque which reads:

THE BOOTHS

First mentioned as
'Les fleshbothes' 1384
one of the two places in town
(with the Northside of
Market Place) reserved for
the sale of
fresh meat.

Almost opposite is a well kept plot with the stone foundations of a Saxon church – the predecessor of All Saints. Erected on the site is a framed description of its history and construction with a picture of what it is considered to have been like in its day. It makes fascinating reading. Excavations at the rear of the cottage bearing the plaque revealed the existence of a cemetery, evidenced by skeletons.

As we mount the hill towards the castle entrance, we think of William the Conqueror during the time of the ravaging of the North. When he was held up at Castleford because of the floodwaters of the river Aire, he did not sit around but explored the area south of the river and spotted the high ground on which

Pontefract now stands. Realizing that it was a great vantage point, he saw that one of his lords should have a stronghold there. That's the story and it is not difficult to believe.

On the right of Micklegate, then, is the entrance to this one-time magnificent castle and the charming little museum. Admission is free to both. The amazing thing about the castle is its enormous size – it covers seven acres, and if one bears in mind the original painting of it done for Charles I, it must have been one of the mightiest in the country. The original painting can be seen in the town museum. Its construction, re-construction and additions were spread over some 600 years – from the eleventh century to the seventeenth century, when the redoubtable Cromwell and his Aide, Fairfax, finally starved the garrison to submission. The things that man destroyed – although one must say that there were a number of historic buildings which came into being during the Common-wealth period. An outstanding piece of workmanship arose, for example, at Newcastle upon Tyne. The seventeenth century Guildhall there which contains the Lord Mayor's parlour has beautifully painted panels with rare topographical views. It is a veritable treasure house.

The largest extant remains of the castle must be the towers of the keep just inside the present entrance; then one enters the huge area, largely grass, but curiosity leads us to the perimeter where a vast area reaching to the plain of York and other directions opens out and emphasizes its position. Here are the remains of the Norman chapel and the later Elizabethan chapel. To the north-west, the remains of the bakehouse and ovens in the enormous kitchen stand over six feet high. An outstanding view of most of the castle can be had from the high ground, the motte near the keep. From here, too, are even better views of the surrounding country than from the eastern perimeter.

Almost in the centre of the greensward is a grate, down which one tends to peer. A well? No. Adjacent to the perimeter path to the west are two trap doors securely padlocked together, which when lifted up reveal a series of steps leading to a magazine, all carved out of the solid sandstone, very deep down. At the very bottom is a large chamber which held the gunpowder. There are also small side chambers where parliamentary prisoners were held. You look up from the main chamber and see daylight coming down a long shaft from the grate in the greensward far above. Parliamentary prisoners' names and dates are carved in the stonework and seem to be almost as clear as they were when first done so many years ago:

JAMES BROVSTON and JOHN GRANT (both 1648)

Cromwell, we are told, was unable to wreck the castle, but after the third onslaught, the Royalists gave in. Subsequently, the people of Pontefract petitioned for the place to be demolished and this was done, alas.

As we leave the 'scant' remains, we pass on our left an attractive building built of ancient stones, which bears the arms of the de Lacy family who were granted vast estates by William I both in Lancashire, centred in Clitheroe, and Yorkshire, centred in Pontefract.

The street we now enter is Micklegate – the one time main thoroughfare of the town and still a busy street – we find on our right a supermarket and a bus station. These were built on the remains of ancient sites, in the 1960s. Under the bus station, in particular, were the Trinities, founded in 1385 when there was a chapel of the Holy Trinity used as a chantry chapel and almshouse for the sick poor. The latter were demolished over a hundred years ago, but excavated in the 1950s prior to the erection of the bus station.

At the top of Micklegate, we reach Horse Fair and Baxtergate on the left. A plaque on the wall tells us that it was the street of the bakers and just round the corner is the Town Hall where there is another plaque:

TOWN HALL AND ASSEMBLY ROOMS

1785

Designed by Bernard Hartley

He, by the way designed the most elegant bridge over the river Aire at Castleford a few years later.

The Town Hall with its clock looks on to the pedestrianised Market Place lined with Georgian and other buildings of various dates. On Wednesdays and Saturdays with the addition of countless market stalls it becomes a scene of very colourful activity with the Butter Cross and Church of St. Giles forming a historic background. The church with its clock tower with vases as pinnacles surmounted by an octagonal lantern stands out for miles around. The original church dates back to the very early twelfth century as a chapel of ease to All Saints, but did not become the parish church until 1789; the chancel is of the nineteenth century and the tower the eighteenth, but the font dates back some 900 years. The nave and east window cannot fail to impress.

The Butter Cross is said to have a close connection with Gibraltar. It appears to have been built with part of the money received as a bribe by a traitor in the Spanish army who led to the British Navy entering Gibraltar and proclaiming it as a British possession. The money used to build the Cross was stated to be specifically mentioned in the traitor's will. Conscience money? Come what may, the Butter Cross still stands there unmoved and at its western side is an ancient pump. Apart from the handle and outlet it is protected by four panels of oak. It is sometimes known as the Elizabethan Pump, but it is not the original one as it was replaced soon after the Butter Cross was built in 1734. At the rear of the pump is a tap which actually issues aqua pura when turned.

What lovely street names abound in Pontefract: Beast Fair, Horse Fair, Baileygate Corn Market, Salterrow, Shoe Market. Let us go down Beast Fair to Southgate and across to the old part of the Infirmary. Under the foundations of the latter and indeed, partly under the present main road, is what is known as the Pontefract Hermitage. It was carved of solid rock by medieval monks, Adam and Robert de Laythorpe from 1386, and consists of living quarters and an Oratory. From the living quarters there is a spiral stone carved staircase leading down to a well. There are no less than 62 steps – 63 if you count the top one! Alas, the copious supply of water no longer exists due to disturbances in the ground when the hospital was built and also because of road construction at the time. In the fourteenth century and indeed for some years after, the water supply in Pontefract was considered to be polluted, and the hermits would sell their very pure water from the well to those who were willing to pay for it.

On ascending the staircase, one notices a human skeleton carved out of the solid rock on the right hand side. There is also a skull on a ledge. The Oratory is entered through another nearby doorway and down some steps – not medieval – in fact part of the roof is supported by a red brick column which in turn supports a hospital wall. When the Oratory became a place to visit in Victorian times, the ladies would be lowered down feet first. A man would be stationed at the bottom to receive the ladies, and found it difficult to refrain from looking upwards to the descending female! In the Oratory is a large and solid stone altar along with stone seats. At the rear of the altar is a carved cross and faintly discernible figures.

It is not surprising that the Hermitage is under lock and key. Access is through the Clinical Psychology Department of the hospital, but it is not readily accessible to the general public. The Pontefract and District Archaeological Society arrange visits from time to time for interested parties, and enquiries can be made through the medium of the town museum.

As we make our way across the road from the hospital, we go up a steep and narrow street, most of which has been rebuilt in old style. There is some interesting stonework in the Cromwell restaurant halfway up. At the top we emerge into the Market Place and note the name of the alley – Maud's Yard. Immediately on our left is a shop (Dorothy Perkins) which is one of the few half-timbered buildings left in the town.

A decayed part of the town has been rebuilt in a pleasant style and at the top is the Museum and a modern library. The museum is quite unique. Here once again is a continental flavour because the curator is Richard Van Riel, Belgian born. The fascinating objects on view are, of course, bound up with Pontefract's history, and what a history! One always wishes one had much more time to spend there. There are even displays of the original very many makes of Pomfret cakes and the tins and packets in which they were sold.

There are now only two makers of the famous liquorice confections in the town: Dunhills at one end and Wilkinsons at the other. Both have factory shops. If the wind is blowing from the north-west, follow your nose from the Corn Market and shortly you will find Dunhills factory and shop with a great assembly of liquorice confections of endless varieties. The other factory, Wilkinsons, is not far from All Saints Church on the Knottingly road. Here again is a factory shop.

Liquorice was brought from the continent by the Crusaders to Pontefract as it was an important monastic centre. At that time, liquorice was used for medicinal purposes. St. Richard's Priory, Cluniac, and St. John's Friary, both at Pontefract have no extant remains, but excavations in 1960 revealed foundations of both. Liquorice took root easily in the district as the soil was sandy and deep, and one George Dunhill, a chemist, first manufactured it as a sweetmeat way back in 1720. It is said that he grew the plant in the castle garths which he rented for the purpose. Eventually, such was the demand that some sixteen firms had made use of it, but the home grown root was nowhere sufficient to meet the demand, so it was imported from Spain and North Africa; British owned firms also had plantations in Russia, Iraq and Turkey. Children in this country who once loved a stick of 'Spanish' have given way in many cases to chocolate. The stamp on Pomfret Cakes, a bird and a gate, is representative of the owl and old castle gate adapted from the Savile Coat of Arms.

It is interesting to note that ninety per cent of the world production of liquorice is now used for flavouring tobacco in America – it also ensures that the tobacco burns evenly.

Whilst on the subject of liquorice and before we leave this historic town, it is thought appropriate to quote Sir John Betjeman:

In the licorice fields at Pontefract
My love and I did meet
And many a burdened licorice bush
Was blooming round our feet:
Red hair she had and golden skin
Her sulky lips were shaped for sin
Her sturdy legs were flannel-slack'd
The strongest legs in Pontefract.

The light and dangling licorice flowers
Gave off the sweetest smells;
From various black Victorian towers
The Sunday evening bells
Came pealing over dales and hills
And tanneries and silent mills
And lowly streets where country stops
And little shuttered corner shops.

She cast her blazing eyes on me
And plucked a licorice leaf;
I was her captive slave and she
My red-haired robber chief.
Oh love! for love I could not speak.
It left me winded, wilting, weak,
And held in brown arms strong and bare

And wound with flaming ropes of hair
22nd. October 1970

One last look at Pomfret: Swales Yard – the wing to the rear of the once three-aisled Manor House – was owned by the Mayor of Pontefract 1561–66 and in 1584 by Alderman Leonard Healaugh. It is half timbered and has been in a ruinous state for far too many years. However, the ugly concrete covered high wall which partially obscured the building on one side has been removed and restoration has taken place. The result is a very attractive inn, The Counting House, with genuine oak beams on the ground floor as well as upstairs. A good place, perhaps, to have one, just one, for the road as we say 'Goodbye' to dear old Pomfret, with its Corn Market and the alleyway, Ream's Terrace, in which The Counting House is situated.

ROTHERHAM

It would be easy to dismiss Rotherham as just another industrial town in what was once the West Riding of Yorkshire . . .

One has not to look too closely at the town to realise how wrong such a description would be. Apart from Stone Age relics, the town has known, in no small measure, the presence of Romans, Saxons and Normans; the Middle Ages have left far more than one would expect. The Dissolution of the Monasteries had great effect here and at a later date, brass, steel and coal brought heavy industry to the area in a big way. In a smaller way, evidence of forges which existed here many centuries ago showed the potential of steel in more modern times.

Although a geological map of Yorkshire will show that Rotherham is in a coal measures area, red sandstone has been quarried in the district; indeed the famous Chantry Bridge and its Chapel of our Lady which crosses the river Don, is built of red sandstone with its warm and inviting look.

Gone are the trams which took you to the surrounding districts; also the many shabby streets of the industrial past have given way to modern buildings and wider roadways. A visitor of 60 years ago would, arriving today and coming from the modern railway station, think that little had changed as he would almost immediately see the Chapel on the Bridge. But wait! Just beyond the Chapel is a huge multi storey car park and the nearby new Rotherham transport interchange, with retail outlets. Striking but . . .

Just walk up Bridgegate, however, the greater part of which is pedestrianised, and you would see that on the right hand it has been widened and completely rebuilt. On the left, there are still one or two really old buildings – seventeenth and eighteenth century – on the upper storey of one is a splendid example of a Venetian window and others of similar beauty. Further up is the ancient hostelry, The Red Lion, but it is somewhat hidden from view by relatively modern Tudor buildings, though quite attractive all the same.

We are now in All Saints Square with the magnificent church standing high up like a guardian of the folk which throng there without having to watch for traffic. Flowers bedeck the Square for most of the year and a fountain completes the picture. The nineteenth century almost wiped out centuries of old Rotherham, but the latter half of the twentieth has almost wiped out the nineteenth century haste, and not a little squalor. The shops in Bridgegate and that with the Venetian window are fully occupied. Here was a large firm of house furnishers – memories of Hastings Happy Homes! Mr James Hastings was responsible for the erection of the now famous clock in what was the original Effingham Square at the upper end of Effingham Street approached from All Saints. He gave the clock with its tower to the town to commemorate the coronation of Geo.V 1911/12. On the modernising of the square, now a huge triangle with roundabout, the clock was

The Chantry Chapel on the Bridge, Rotherham

removed, along with its weights which needed a fourteen foot shaft. It was eventually replaced in a somewhat different position nearby but without the need for weights and a deep shaft. There it stands, as good as new in blue and gold, to tell the time from all four angles, in exactly the same style as the famous clock on the promenade at Douglas, Isle of Man. The seats nearby were given by Mr Hastings' grandson.

The name Effingham reminds us that much of the land hereabouts was owned by the Earl of Effingham. Also it was only in 1851 that he was legally entitled to grant long leases for development of the town. The street names around here, it will be noticed, are Frederick, Henry, Howard – they were sons of the Effingham family.

Leaving the clock behind us, we make our way up a steep hill to Clifton Park and its mansion, now a fascinating museum. It was opened in 1891 by the then Prince of Wales; after great improvements and a greater display of fascinating displays, it was reopened in May 1991 – 100 years later, again by Royalty, this time by Queen Elizabeth II. It can be reached on foot in six or seven minutes at a brisk pace. Just inside the Park entrance is a war memorial which surely cannot fail to bring one to a halt to pay homage to those who gave their lives for our freedom and pray that we all, in recognising their sacrifice, share responsibility and duties, as well as rights, in an endeavour to try and make a better world.

Towards the top of the Park is a great rockery and immediately behind it are the remains of a rampart which we associate with the Civil War defences of the town which was largely parliamentarian. The Earl of Newcastle, the great Royalist, stormed Rotherham in 1643, but without success, and in the end King Charles I passed through Rotherham by way of the Chantry Bridge a defeated man, and was finally beheaded in 1649. Just on the east side of the museum is more evidence of Rotherham's historic past. Here you will see Roman columns in plenty and a portico, well set out among the lawns and trees. These remains were discovered some one and a half miles up stream from the town when industrial development took place and were re-erected here for all to see. It appears that the original site, Templeborough, was an important Roman station with baths in its heyday. We are fortunate to see part of it as it stood, even though it is in a new and, let us hope, a permanent situation.

Inside the museum there is an interest for everybody – geology, life in Ancient Britain especially around Rotherham, Tudor days, Roman and Norman times, Victorian furniture and the Industrial Revolution. In the Roman section is a huge amphora for holding wine (without a pointed base), several Roman altars and beehive querns. To complete the picture are very beautifully sculptured memorial stones. The first one of note is inscribed in Latin which when translated means:

TO THE DIVINE SHADES
CENTUSMUS
A SOLDIER OF THE 4TH

COHORT OF GAULS
MELESUS ERECTED THIS

On the left of this is another memorial stone, unfortunately headless, dedicated to another soldier of the 4th cohort; he was the husband – age 40, of Flavia Peregrina, a most devoted wife who erected it. One other memorial stands on the right, but no name is visible. It is some four feet high of carved stone.

In another part of the museum are very beautiful specimens of Rockingham porcelain and china once made at nearby Swinton. Such was the fame of Bramalds that they produced a set of 200 pieces for William IV, examples of such works of art are there for all to see. The Rhinoceros Vase on show at the foot of the staircase, which was produced for the Earl Fitzwilliam in 1826 defies description. The golden rhinoceros crowns the top of the vase from which it takes its name. The size and exquisite workmanship cannot fail to impress. The great pity of it is the Rockingham factory is no more. The firm went out of business many years ago.

Turning around from the past, outside the museum we are confronted by an enormous and towering erection of modern flats.

It is quite outstanding and somehow fits in well with the new widened roads, traffic lights and endless fast flowing traffic. We hear today of Robin Hood country, Shakespeare country, Herriot country, but over a hundred years ago Sir Walter Scott, the great novelist chose the neighbourhood near Rotherham which became known as Ivanhoe country for the chief scenes of his novel of that name. So, if we have a look at the district from the top of that not unattractive block of flats, it will conjure up in our minds Ivanhoe country stretching far and wide from there to Doncaster, as well as Conisbrough Castle, Tickhill, Wentworth, giving life to scenes peopled with monks, knights in armour, Jews, jugglers, palmers, outlaws, serfs.

In this connection it is worthwhile to slip away from Rotherham and that high rise set of flats and enter Ivanhoe country proper and have a walk along one or two of Conisbrough's ancient streets, down one of which is the Parish Church of St. Peter. The present building embodies much of the remains of the Saxon Minster built c.750 A.D., the oldest building in South Yorkshire. In the twelfth century, the Saxon church was remodelled and in the fifteenth century the chancel was extended eastward. Outside this is very apparent as the stone employed appears to be cream coloured limestone as opposed to the rest of the building which is of a hard variety of white limestone. Conisbrough is situated on the high ground formed by the band of limestone which stretches from the river Tees to the Don. The church is full of interest, including fragments of fifteenth century glass to be seen in the window of the south wall. There is also a stone tomb chest found in the church yard, dated c.1140. Its lid is covered with carved medallions enclosing fighting knights, winged beasts and signs of the zodiac. On one side, a warrior fights a dragon and a bishop with crozier stands aside him.

You go down the hill and take the second turning after the church and a very

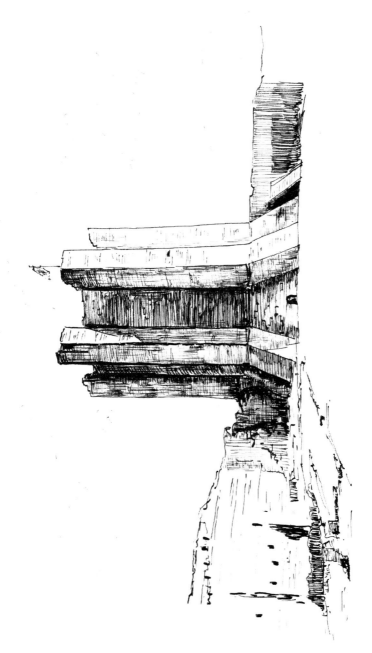

The Keep at Conisbrough Castle

impressive sight appears before you. Perched on an enormous mound with ditches around it is Conisbrough Castle. The ruins are far beyond one's expectations. No small wonder that Sir Walter Scott got inspiration for his novel. As we enter the Visitors' Centre, we soon learn that the enormous keep houses an audio-visual experience of epic proportions. Once inside the keep, you travel back in time to a day in 1417 A.D. when the castle was under seige by the Earl of Lancaster's men. You feel the atmosphere as the drama unfolds showing how John de Warrenne abducted Lancaster's wife, holding her hostage within the castle, and witness the turmoil this causes throughout the household.

Whilst the keep is the principal attraction, the curtain walls of the inner ward and the towers cannot fail to impress the visiting tourist. The top of the keep, some 90 feet above the inner ward, is reached by a series of stone steps. On the way up by means of recently constructed outside steps, the main entrance is reached, and so we enter the first floor from which one can peer down through the grille into the basement. The next floor is reached by means of a stone staircase built within the thickness of the outer wall which is 15 feet thick. Once in the circular room we learn that it was the Lord's chamber with its enormous fireplace. More stone stairs lead to the Lord's private chamber with a chapel built within the outer walls. The latter should not be missed as it is almost intact. The roof, another stone staircase, has been restored and one can walk almost round it. The views in all directions reveal the importance of the site and relatively unspoiled hilly and wooded country around. The old village and its church among the trees provide a lovely picture.

Setting foot again in the inner ward, one is impressed by the fact that whilst all the rooms in the keep are circular, even the basement, the massive buttresses, all six of them, suggest a far from circular building and along with the circular part of it are splayed outward giving great strength. This is shown by the fact that the keep has stood the ravages of time and weather for some 800 years; only at the very top has a little restoration of stonework been necessary.

There is a narrow footpath right round the base of the stonework of the castle with the ditch on one side of you, whilst there is another walk on the outer perimeter of the ditch.

The Manor of Conisbrough belonged to King Harold before the conquest, and William gave it to William de Warren who built the castle. We can be sure that the present ruins were not due to Oliver Cromwell because the castle had already fallen into disrepair about one hundred years before his time!

However, Conisbrough Castle is now well maintained through the joint efforts of English Heritage, The Ivanhoe Trust and Doncaster Council. Ivanhoe is thus far from being forgotten because you will see that along the High Street is a prominent house called Ivanhoe Lodge, and you can even hire an Ivanhoe Cab!!

Back in Rotherham town at the Hastings Clock and along Effingham Street, we reach the cathedral-like church of All Saints. The town and its church were mentioned in The Domesday Book of 1074, but be assured that it was a small church which stood on that elevated position overlooking the dwellings which existed at that time and dated as far back as 937 A.D. A larger Norman church on the same site with transepts was built in the twelfth century, but the church we see to-day dates from 1483 being almost re-erected by the monks of Rufford Abbey, Nottinghamshire.

We enter the church by the south door and are at once amazed at the immensity and beauty. The time spent and the dedication of those who did the building is once more a wonderful example of their utmost faith. Norman stonework is in evidence in the nave and chancel as well as in part of the east wall. The beautiful Chapel of Jesus in the south choir aisle was erected by Thoms Rotherham in 1480 when he was Bishop of Lincoln. Thomas was born in College Street near the church and went to Rotherham Grammar School, Eton and Cambridge, entered the church and eventually became Archbishop of York. He never forgot Rotherham and through him the Chantry Chapel on the bridge was built. He founded the College of Jesus in the town – gone for ever, *vide* Henry VIII, but a most attractive relic of the college is to be seen at the town's Boston Park which will be visited later.

The roof of the nave of All Saints with very fine bosses consists of the oak that was placed there 500 years ago. It is said that oak, provided that dry or wet rot does not occur, hardens with age, so perhaps that dreaded little beetle seems to have been kept at bay for this reason. Let us hope the oak will harden still more! A feature of the nave is the series of diamond shaped pillars – probably unique. Before we leave this wonderful House of God, it is well worth looking at two special memorials. The first is that of Samuel Buck, eminent lawyer who died in 1803: it was sculptured by the well known R.J.A. Flaxman whose perfect workmanship is more than apparent. The eighteenth century shop in Bridgegate which features the Venetian style window was the town house of Samuel Buck's grandfather and indeed where the former also lived – they were both lawyers. The other memorial is a masterpiece of wood carving, the Angel of the Annunciation on the stall of the one time Provost of Jesus College.

Tearing ourselves away, we ask if we may have the key of the Chantry Chapel on the Bridge and then go down Bridgegate and across the road to it. Here we see the Chapel of our Lady, the presence of which is due to the efforts, not to mention the expense borne by Thomas Rotherham. After completion it was used by travellers over the bridge to ask for God's blessing upon their journeys, and masses were said for the repose of the dead. Alas, from its closure by Henry VIII, it had a chequered career. At first it was converted into an almshouse, but in 1779, it became a deputy constable's house and prisoners were kept in the crypt. For some time after that it was used solely as a constable's residence. In 1888 it was turned into a newsagent's and tobacconist's shop. Fortunately the people of Rotherham were unhappy at this desecration of such a sacred place, but it took many years and much hard work before the Chapel was restored and rededicated in 1924. Since then, further restoration has taken place. Of special

The original doorway of Jesus College

note is the east window, incorporated in the stained glass of which is the Coat of Arms of Thomas Rotherham. The window also reflects quite vividly God's presence throughout the Chapel's history as well as the little statue of Our Lady. The latter is modern, and replaces one which was removed at the Dissolution in 1547.

On entering, one is immediately impressed by the simple beauty of the place, duly complemented by the obvious care and attention given to keeping it immaculate. A descent into the crypt is made through a trap door in the floor near the entrance. Stone steps lead one down to find it is divided into compartments. There are graffiti and initials of prisoners on an ancient door which leans against a stone partition. Substantial strap hinges, though rusty, still remain on the door in which there is a spy-hole at eye level. A prison cell indeed and a grim reminder of past ages, Ascending the steps again, just before emerging into the Chapel, one is brought back with a jerk to the 1990s by the sight of an up to date electricity fuse box and switchboard! It is good to note that Holy Communion is celebrated each Tuesday in the Chapel at 11 a.m.

Today it stands high and dry above the river, but still on a small island, and integral with the old bridge. However, the course of the Don has been diverted some yards to the south leaving the four pointed arches and the Chapel's foundations out of the water in normal conditions. The southern abutment has been strengthened and connection with the new modern style bridge is made by means of a half arch. It seems a pity that some of the cutwaters of the old bridge have not been replaced. The northern end of the old bridge is still coincident with the old sidewalk of the road from which the Chapel can be entered as well as from the south side.

After returning the key of the Chapel at All Saints, we make our way into High Street and Moorgate Street. Going up hill we pass the new Town Hall of Rotherham on our left – a handsome building of the palest of grey masonry, almost white in the bright sunshine – and then proceed up Moorgate Road for about a mile, passing many dignified houses until the Belvedere Hotel is reached. Here we see a huge sweeping area of greensward surrounded by a belt of mature trees. Overlooking this is a magnificent square-towered entrance of the Thomas Rotherham College, a further memorial to that most remarkable man. Continuing past the side entrance to the college, we carry on up the road to Boston Park entrance. Very soon the "castle" comes into view. It is a crenellated shooting lodge – now occupied by a horticulturist. It was built by the Earl of Effingham who felt strongly that the American War of Independence was unjust and when his regiment was ordered to America he resigned his commission rather than fight a cause which he thought was wrong. The "Castle" was named in memory of the Boston Tea Party, although a number of shooting parties were held there and wine was drunk, tea was forbidden!

Around the castle are over 20 acres of hill top paths from which one has stupendous views of the Don and Rother valleys, not what the Countryside Commission would call beautiful, but industry, that vital element upon which so many livelihoods depend, has got to be somewhere. Going down a gently sloping path between some hundred yards from the castle, one has a most pleasant surprise. At each side among the trees are some extraordinary large stones, some appear to be carved and some just odd-shaped. Suddenly on our left is a reddish brown sandstone cliff face extending for about 100 yards and surmounted by trees. Set in a recess in the cliff is the original doorway of Jesus College which was rescued in the nineteenth century from development in College Lane and College Street. It is something like twelve feet high and still displays the dedicated workmanship of the men who built it so many centuries ago. Flower beds abound, pathways this way and that. There is even a bowling green in a great setting. Flowers grow at the base of the cliff and add to its charm. On the way out and near the entrance to the castle is a coat of arms carved out of a large block of stone incorporated in the stone wall. It bears the legend: 'Incorporated July 1836'.

Back in town to Main Street which leads us over a massive bridge across the river, but just before going over the bridge, we enter Market Street and thence to Corporation Street and the new Riverside Precinct which occupies a very ancient site, that of Rotherham's corn mill mentioned in the Domesday Book. As was usual in those far off days, all tenants of the manor had to grind their corn there. The weir which held up the water to power the mill is still to be seen.

One cannot conclude our story of Rotherham and Ivanhoe Country without quoting from Miss Dorothy Greene FSA:

"As one stands today on the old Rotherham Bridge, gazing on the busy scene dominated now, as of yore, by the great church of All Saints, one's mind swings back, the hum of modern traffic fades and for a moment one sees again that 'fair Rotherham' which to our ancestors was a 'greate towne', sees again the sunlight fall softly on the trees which line the Don, the sparkle of silver water, the flash of trout as he darts beneath the shadow of the bridge, and hear the sharp tramp of horses' feet as a procession, gay and vivid, winds over the narrow bridge. And what a procession Time has led across that bridge! Flash of purple and gold as Thomas Rotherham rides by on his richly caparisoned mule; more sombre hues as another Archbishop of York, Cardinal Wolsey, rides sadly by, a fallen and broken man, in 1529; jingle of arms as the escort surrounding Mary, Queen of Scots, passes by and the stern tramp of Ironsides, as Cromwell's men conduct her grandson, King Charles, to Rotherham on his journey to Whitehall and death. Later, softer things claim our attention, and a poetic figure leans upon the parapet as Ebenezer Elliott, the Corn Law Rhymer, watches the dappled trout and flash of birds in flight, and his contemporary, Ebenezer Rhodes, pauses on the Bridge to watch the rays of the setting sun gild the great Church, rising above the huddled roofs of houses and the stately elms which stand on the 'river's trembling edge'.

On that same Bridge in the Festival Year of 1951 we pause awhile to dream, and then enter the little shrine where once again praise is raised to Almighty God".

As the Millennium approaches may that little shrine still welcome those who pause awhile to dream and again raise praise to Almighty God.

CAWOOD

"Cawood, where's that?" many will exclaim.

After its romantic course through the Yorkshire dale which bears its name the Wharfe quietly meanders through meadows and pastures and joins the Ouse a very short distance upstream from the little town of Cawood which is no more than 10 miles from the great City of York. The Ouse is tidal at Cawood and whilst there has never been an historic bridge over the river, a ferry has existed from time immemorial until 1872 when a steel bridge was built. Today a lofty tower stands in the middle and barriers drop down when the bridge is about to swing open for the passage of river traffic.

Long before 1872 the trade route between the Scandinavian countries and Ireland came by way of the Humber, Ouse and Cawood. Wouldn't those traders have loved the Aire and Calder and the Leeds and Liverpool canals! Years later the Romans used the ford at Cawood on their journey from Castleford to York. Athelstan, the first king of all England, gave the manors of Cawood and Sherburn to Wolfstan, Archbishop of York to commemorate his victory over the Scots in the tenth century. The Normans strengthened Cawood and from then on it became the seat of the Archbishops of York and a regular second home for royalty.

Cawood is situated at the point where the York to Sherburn road crosses the road from Tadcaster to Selby. In the town the roads bear such names as Thread-gold Lane and Old Boys School Lane. Then there are interwoven alleys and courtyards, some of which are a pleasure to the eye, and indeed, to the artist and photographer. Mellow brick and stone lintels, cornices and mullions add to the charm.

This little town was, in the past, on an important waterway and most goods were carried to and from it by water traffic – hence wheeled traffic was infrequent. There are many inns – Cawood was a good and convenient stopping place. Even today there are six.

The Castle is a must, and just round the corner from the High Street stands the original and very imposing innerside of the Gatehouse with a spacious green between it and the road. The latter was made just over a hundred years ago to supersede the narrow Old Road which led to Selby. The new road crosses what must surely have been the inner ward. The north outer wall would then be quite near the river. The white stone gatehouse is all that remains of the original castle. It is well kept and makes a very attractive picture. Above the massive oak doors of the former entrance there are a living-room and a kitchen; above these there is a bedroom and a bathroom. A romantic place in which one may stay for a holiday, self-catering. The property is owned by the Landmark Trust, so one can rent the rooms and think that as far back as 1300, Edward I with his second wife Margaret stayed there too.

Dick Turpin and his horse, the famous Black Bess, crossed the river at Cawood when riding from London to York.

For a brief history lesson about the enthronement of George Neville as Archbishop of York, one might well visit the Ferry Inn. There on a large plaque, is the astounding menu of the Great Feast to celebrate his coming enthronement. On 15th January 1466, St. Maurice's Day, Cawood Castle saw the greatest feast ever recorded. it is said that over 8,000 people gathered there from miles around, and many came from York to participate in the event, which lasted several days. More than 1,000 were employed to cook and serve the food, seven courses in all. Included in the menu were 500 stags, buck and roes, 1,000 muttons, 2,000 geese, 4,000 pasties of venison, 3,000 cold baked custards and 2,000 hot custards, 300 tuns of ale and 100 tuns of wine.

George Neville's effort only enhanced his reputation for a short time and after seven years he was stripped of everything and sent to prison in France, having incurred the King's displeasure.

Cardinal Wolsey, who, after being made Chancellor of England by Henry VIII, fell out of favour with the King by agreeing with him over the divorce of Katherine of Aragon, but agreeing also with the Pope's opinion, was sent to Cawood in 1530. After settling in at Cawood, three weeks before his enthronement as Archbishop of York, Wolsey was arrested by the Earl of Northumberland on a charge of high treason. The rest of the sad story of Wolsey we all know.

The year 1646 saw the end of Cawood staging the splendour of Royalty and Archbishops. The castle was voted by the House of Commons as redundant.

Cawood Castle

Much of the stone was removed and used to build the entrance of Bishopthorpe, the Archbishop of York's palace – still, of course, in use.

Cawood is the point where the old Bishop's Dyke joins the Ouse. The Dyke was built to run from Sherburn to the town, and its waters provided power for corn mills. At one time Huddlestone Quarry, near Sherburn, sent limestone via the Dyke to Cawood and thence from the Ouse to York for building purposes, especially for repairing and indeed building some of the Minster. The route followed by the Dyke can still be traced, especially near the Bishopdike road leading to Sherburn.

Now we return to the High Street and turn right into the Old Road near the river, and if we are there at the right time, barges can be seen taking paper to York for the *Yorkshire Evening Press* and not wasting much time cutting their way through the water of that historic river. Other water-going vessels which need the swing bridge to come into action, give the look-out man a signal about a mile away to notify their approach. Before the Old Road joins the new, we leave it and pass along a unique row of attractive houses, all appear to have a different character. It is called Water Row and dates from the late eighteenth and early nineteenth century. The greater parts of their gardens are across the little road and slope down to the river. At the end of the Row, we join the new road and are soon confronted by the tower of All Saints parish church. It has a complete Norman doorway and original Norman stones and Saxon gravestones can be seen in the structure of the church. The entrance is facing the road and there is a notice which informs the visitor where the key can be obtained if the church is closed. Inside there is a medieval font, an ancient stone used for holding candles, and among many items of interest is the Jacobean pulpit. There is also a bust of George Mountain who rose from being a local farmer's son to be the Dean of Westminster, Bishop of Lincoln and then Bishop of London. The sad note, however, is that only one day after he had been enthroned as Archbishop of York he tragically died.

The altar was discovered in the floor of the vestry over 70 years ago and restored. It is of stone with five crosses representing the wounds of Christ. The story goes that the altar was hidden in the floor to prevent Cromwell's men destroying it.

Outside the clock is placed in an unusual position on the tower and it is interesting to note that some 150 years ago it was bought from Selby Abbey at a cost of £20, and the gentleman who was given the job of winding it up was paid no less than 10 shillings per annum!

And so Cawood, proud of its long history and once regarded as the Windsor of the North stands serenely beside the Ouse – so many people quite unaware of its existence, let alone its momentous history.

As we make our way to Selby, we notice that pigeons coo and perch on the raised numerals of the church clock – obviously, in Cawood at least, oblivious of time . . .

SELBY

For once we have a town without an authentic history of stoneage man, Romans, Danes or Vikings. Unique? The area around Selby is reported to have been lacking in permanent habitation before the Conquest. This is easy to imagine as Selby is only 20 feet above sea level and about 35 miles from the coast, and also the river Ouse, in rainy seasons was wont to overflow its banks in that very flat area, especially when meeting a flood tide when almost every river in Yorkshire emptied its waters into it. This would, of course, cause the vast area of land around Selby to be marshy and almost featureless. It is thought, however, that Danes and Vikings may well have founded tiny settlements here and there.

Even the Ouse which flows south from York then turns west only to make a sudden U-turn on approaching Selby and makes its way east!

However, a talented French monk, Benedict, had a vision in which St. Germanus appeared and commanded him to venture to Britain and establish a religious house in the north of England. He reached Salisbury, but the need to travel north was paramount. Having reached that great bend in the Ouse, he settled at a spot, a sandy knoll, high up on the river bank and built a rude dwelling in which he could pay homage to God and try to encourage the odd traveller to join him. This is said to have been in 1069, some three years after the redoubtable William I did his conquering. The latter, hearing about Benedict and his humble home and cross, decided that a monastery be founded there and that land be granted to him on both sides of the river. And so, over the years, a small religious house came into being some 150 yards away from the river where Benedict first erected his cross. Selby thus came about.

It is interesting to note that Henry I, the youngest son of William I was born at Selby, when his mother, Matilda, was on her way to York. It is nice to think that Henry encouraged the development of the Abbey by means of grants of land and funds because it was the place of his birth. This is said to be true, but it is also said that he thought that a grand monastic establishment in an area where there were possible groups, though small, who still resisted his father's conquest, could be finally subdued. The fact remains that the Abbey prospered and developed as a result. Today, nearly 900 years later, the very same stones used in the building of the church can still be seen on its north side. Abbot Hugh, one of Benedict's most famous successors actually carried stone and lime himself in the twelfth century. One wonders who put the very first stone in place and where. Perhaps he did both!!

The result is plain. Selby Abbey is one of the finest Romanesque churches in England. Today, the Abbey, a parish church since Henry VIII's time, is for many the main attraction in the town. The grounds on the south side in which it stands were once the site of the Chapter House, the Cloister Court and a thirteenth century chamber. Sadly only a few stones here and there

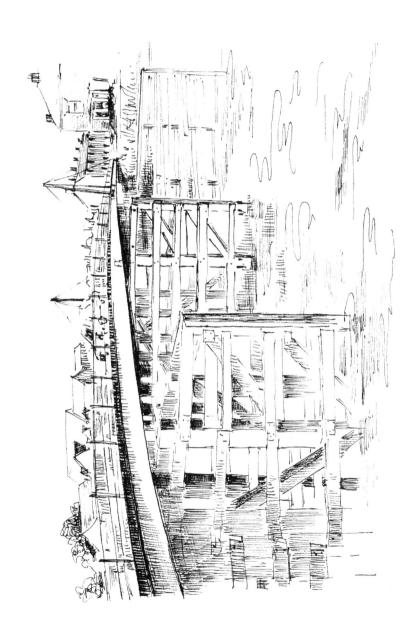

Modernised wooden bridge at Selby

Selby Abbey and Market Cross

remain. To the west was a Gate House which was unfortunately dismantled in 1797.

Inside, at the end of the nave on the south side, is a most unusual pillar. Unlike the other pillars, it is carved from top to bottom with a criss-cross design and is called Abbot Hugh's Pillar. Even the small corbels of the abacus are uniquely carved. The carved stonework in and around the Retro Choir cannot fail to impress one on account of the fantastic workmanship of those men who created it – a wonderful sight when the sun is shining through the East Window.

The great cross on the choir screen is a remarkable work of art done some 90 years ago. Then there is the Washington Shield in one of the south clerestory windows of the choir. It is said that the heraldic arms of the Washington family, stars and stripes, are the original idea of the national flag of the U.S.A. Prior of Durham 1416, John Wessington, was an ancestor of George Washington whose family lived at Washington Old Hall, County Durham. Washington Old Hall was visited by President Carter along with Prime Minister, James Callaghan in 1977. New York in 1664 was called New Amsterdam. Charles II questioned this and sent his fleet to assert his rights, but the Dutch, anticipating this, built a wall across the island. This wall is perpetuated by the Stock Exchange in New York by calling it Wall Street. Nevertheless the British won the day and renamed the settlement New York. Selby Abbey had a close connection with Durham in times past.

The sedilia in the Sanctuary, dated from the late fourteenth century, is comparable with the Neville screen at Durham – the main features are the wonderfully carved pinnacles.

The walk, high up in the clerestory, both north and south, and the choir gallery, possess unusual architectural features. They are quite safe, but gaining them is said to be 'rather dangerous' owing to insecure footholds on the way up. In fact at the present time it is regarded as unsafe for access by the general public. Lucky is he who ever ascends those steps to obtain one of the most profound views in Christendom.

As we go westward, on the north aisle there are several stands with illustrated short stories of the varied periods in the history of Selby itself. These fit in well with the history of the Abbey, and give one much food for thought. There are Pickworth tombs, one on each side of the west end. Hugh de Pickworth, carved in stone, forms the tomb cover and shows his shield with the picts still clearly visible. He fought for Edward II in Scotland way back in 1310. His wife Margery is also carved in stone on the tomb cover on the other side.

Selby is in the Diocese of York, but has a suffragan Bishop, and at the time of writing is The Rt. Revd. H.V. Taylor, its Vicar being the Revd. James A. Robertson, both of whom, together with Lady Martin Fitzalan Howard are to be commended for their unflagging efforts to keep this lovely and quite unique House of God in good structural condition. York, quite rightly, claims very, very many visitors not only from the U.K. but from all parts of the world, but Selby seems to suffer. One wonders if the words 'Selby Abbey' conjures up in visitors' minds, 'just another ruin'. If so, the illusion is immediately dispelled when a visit is made, because that cathedral-like psalm in stone, shining white in the sunshine, can be described as one of the greatest architectural jewels in the north of England. It is free for all to enter, and it is a privilege to make a voluntary contribution towards its upkeep. To describe all its treasures would take a whole book, so the answer is to make a visit. It is only 13 miles from York by way of a southbound fine motor road.

The Abbey has had its share of disasters. Way back in the middle of the sixteenth century came the Dissolution; then the Civil War during which fighting actually took place in Selby streets and the Abbey suffered damage. In 1690 the great central tower collapsed, and in 1906, a disastrous fire did untold damage – the roof was open to the sky – but financial assistance was so forthcoming that not only the nave and choir were renewed before the end of 1912, but also the south transept which had been in ruins since 1690. At the same time the north transept was restored. So well has the whole work of restoration been done that many visitors would not realize what had really happened.

Before the advent of the industrial revolution in the West Riding of Yorkshire, Selby town had had its moments, apart from its part in the Civil War. After a period of stagnation, it became an important focal point for the export and import trade. Pack horses brought goods from the West Riding and indeed elsewhere to the port of Selby and thence by ship to Hull, but with the opening of the canal from the river Aire at Haddlesey to Selby and the railway to the town from Leeds in 1834, it became more of a focal point than ever, especially when the railway was extended to Hull soon after. It really became an important railway centre when trains to King's Cross, Doncaster to York and beyond passed through Selby. The ship building industry which had long been localised in the town prospered more than ever, until the little village of Goole some miles down river became the terminus of the Knottingley canal which by-passed Selby. There was also deeper water at Goole and a railway direct from Wakefield. More and more goods to and from the West Riding went via Goole and the population of the latter rose rapidly, until now it is something like 18,000 as against Selby's 12,000. Even the famous wooden bridge built in 1791/2, the only bridge which crossed the Ouse between York and the sea which furthered Selby's importance, did not stop little Goole from growing.

In spite of all this and the decline in ship building, other industries have sprung up in Selby; flour milling, oil and cake milling, rice processing, mushroom growing, chemical manufacturing and paper making. Very important is the coalfield, now one of the most modern in Europe. It consists of five shaft mines connected with remote controlled underground conveyors to the drift mine at Gascoigne Wood where coal is brought up to the surface. In addition, Selby has been, for so many years, a market town and an agricultural centre. Market Day on a Monday presents a very animated scene with the West Front of the Abbey to east, the Londesborough Arms Hotel to the north and to the west is the ancient market cross.

Why 'Londesborough Arms'? It was named after Lord Londesborough who purchased the manor of Selby some 150 years ago.

From the market place, we go along the long and very wide main street, Gowthorpe, it curves slightly towards the south-west and at its end is the Roman Catholic Church of St. Mary with its spire which can be seen in the distance from the market cross. On the way, on the left is a short street with its name carved in the stonework of the corner building, Audus Street. An unusual name? We find that among the rich merchants and ship owners of the eighteenth and nineteenth centuries was one John Audus who came from Robin Hood's Bay in 1771. He demolished the slums near the Abbey and built what is now The Crescent with the present public park nearby. His son, James, was just as enthusiastic as his father in the well-being of the town and as one goes down Audus street, the prominent square tower of St. James Church stands out clearly. As this church was built and endowed entirely at James Audus' expense, it is not surprising to see the little street bearing his name.

Further along Gowthorpe on the same side of the road are some not unattractive homes 'for the aged and pious' where they could end their days rent free. Again, James Audus was responsible for their erection and maintenance. Here and there, along a number of roads and streets there are little gems of Georgian houses, so often unnoticed as one drives along in great haste.

Let us now return to the Abbey and to The Crescent leading to the historic Ouse river. For centuries Selby folk and travellers crossed the river by ferry until 200 years ago, when the famous wooden swing bridge was built. It was a quite remarkable achievement of civil engineering and the best surviving bridge of its kind in England, also one of the earliest swing bridges in Europe – it was carried on ball bearings! After 180 years of constant and increasing motor traffic, the bridge had had its day, and a new steel framed structure replaced it, but still exacted the toll until September 1991. It still swings when required as heretofore though not so frequently as it did when far more river traffic made its way up and down river. Only the central part of the bridge swivels and the stout wooden supports are still to be seen.

Instead of crossing the swing bridge we go down Ousegate, where on the river bank a pleasant resting place with seats has been created in place of a derelict staith. Then passing under the railway, we come to the Selby canal which, as previously mentioned, connected Selby with the river Aire and brought river traffic from the West Riding. The railway, and later modern road traffic brought about the canal's stagnation. However, the side of the canal south of the railway promises to be an attractive spot for boating with overnight moorings, along with a landscaped park with seating and car parking. Possible completion in 1998.

We now turn about and return to the swing bridge, dash across the never-ending stream of traffic and turn up Churchill and cross the Selby Dam, a long and deep sided canal-like waterway from the west on its way to the Ouse, a wonderful drain for that huge area of once often flooded marshy land.

Proceeding from Churchill and Water Lane into Micklegate, we come to Millgate. Here, the new is integrated with the old in a most attractive way. There is an old inn, and an ancient chapel, St. Michael's 1699, rebuilt 1903, new dwellings, Friendship Court and Firth Mews, for example, which cannot fail to attract attention by their thoughtful arrangement. Back in Micklegate and Finkle Street, we once again enter the market place.

Today, not unlike countless other towns in Britain, Selby possesses Shopping Malls, Super Markets and a Civic Centre with large car parks, but in spite of this the town still remains unique.

As we return to the West Riding (West Yorkshire!), we pass through mile upon mile of golden corn fields and potato fields of a rich dark green colour, and realise that over the centuries the overflowing rivers of the Yorkshire Dales carried down to the Ouse in this area of level ground countless tons of mud and decayed vegetable matter. The result has been the making of a deeper and richer soil century after century. Perhaps we ought to thank, also, the men who dug the Selby Dam which helped to drain that once 'soggy plain' of the past. We cannot forget, also, the stirring events in the town's history extending to more than 900 years. The thoughts of 900 years brings back the memory of the occasion when Queen Elizabeth II came to Selby in April 1969 for the Maundy Service at the Abbey, the first time ever that Maundy Thursday was celebrated in a parish church, especially as it was on the 900th. anniversary of the erecting of The Cross on the banks of the Ouse nearby.

BEVERLEY

One of the most striking ways of approach is surely from the west with the famous race course one one's left. Another is along the road which straddles the golf course and enters the town where Newbegin Bar once stood. From this road, with the vast greensward and trees in the foreground, that priceless gem, the Minster, stands out in great relief, especially just before sunset, its twin towers reaching up to the Heavens.

A land of promise indeed, but before we hurry along to see the countless treasures the town has to offer let us have a look at the extraordinary golf clubhouse. The large dark looking tower in its midst was formerly a windmill in which the famous flour of Beverley was produced by one James Thorsk until a hundred years ago. The five sails and works, alas, are no more, and so the tall dark remains form part of the club house.

Both these sporting areas are part of what is known as Westwood which was 'given' to the town of Beverley by Archbishop Neville in 1380 at a rent of £5 per annum and gave freedom of movement to all who visit the area, but watch out for flying golf balls! That is, if one is in the southern half. The race course dates back as far back as 1767 when organized racing became the 'thing' at Beverley.

The most attractive entrance to the town must surely be by way of the North Bar – the only one of four now standing. The other three were demolished nearly two centuries ago, long before the National Trust, Ministry of Works, Department of the Environment or English Heritage were thought of. The mellow red brick North Bar (facing north-west) was rebuilt as far back as 1409, and within is a plaque on the wall bearing the following legend:

NORTH BAR

THIS BAR IS THE ONLY REMAINING ONE
OF THOSE WHICH FORMERLY GUARDED
THE MAIN ENTRANCES TO THE TOWN. IT
WAS BUILT BY THE TOWN COUNCIL IN
1409 AT A COST OF £96 – 0 – 11½ *d*

N.B. The Beverley and District Civic Society
Say that the cost was £96 – 17 – 4½ !!

The other Bars, Newbegin (West) was taken down in 1790, and Kelgate Bar (South) was removed in 1808 as it was too low for the then modern transport of hay to get through. Finally, the one time Norwood Bar at the end of Hengate was taken down during the same period. In Hengate, near the Bar, stands the oldest public house, seventeenth century, some of it earlier, which is known as 'Nellie's' after its one time owner, though the model of a white horse over the

North Bar Within, Beverley

door proclaims its real name. It is a must for those interested in old inns and possesses a unique atmosphere. No mock Tudor old beams here, let it be said, but there are many separate snugs and rooms. Even today, it is illuminated by gas although electricity is laid on, and evidence of modernising in Victorian and Edwardian times is apparent. Beer pumps give it away. It is said that the inn was a place where voters were influenced generously by the Tories. Next door is the sunken entrance to a one time wine bar, known as 'Ardens' – it is still known by that name. Jane Arden, a member of the Arden family of Beverley in the eighteenth century, was a friend of Mary Wollstonecraft of 'A Vindication of the Rights of Women' fame.

Let us now take a little notice of the one and only still standing Bar. The immediate approach road is known as North Bar Without and once through it is known as North Bar Within. It presents a colourful sight both from without and within. The arms are those of Michael Warton, impaled with his wife, Susannah, the daughter of a peer. The massive door of oak, still on its hinges, is always open and rests in its own recess. It was taken down in recent years for examination and found to be as sound as ever. Traffic lights control the passage of traffic. The handsome building just outside the Bar was the residence of James Elwell – father of the well known Beverley artist, 1887 – 1958. He was an R.A. and his paintings in and around Beverley can be seen in the many art shops in the town. A collection of his works is on show in the Beverley Art Gallery. Entering the town again, there is, on the right, St. Mary's Court, a fifteenth century timbered building, one of the few left. It is said that Henry VIII's antiquary, John Leland, must have been very impressed by it and other buildings of a similar nature and caused him to describe Beverley as "large and well builded of wood".

Ahead stands the elaborate Market Cross (1712) quite serenely overlooking the animated scene of the Market in which on a Saturday the stalls fill all available space. The condition of the Cross evidences that much care and attention is given to it. Its roof is supported by eight columns and sports eight urns as well as a lantern and pinnacle. It is a splendid successor to the original which existed so many years before 1712.

On our left stands the great church of St. Mary which could be, to the uninitiated visitor, mistaken for the Minster. It dates back to 1120 and was the subject of enlargement and development for something like 400 years. The treasures it contains are innumerable. It has two remarkable features, the first is the vestry, access being gained by a short stone staircase. Its ceiling is of wood and painted showing the constellations and the sun. Underneath this feature which was once a chapel, is the most comfortable vaulted crypt one could find. It is carpeted, furnished and heated and is used as a quiet room.

Another feature is the War Memorial Door. It is quite unique and commemorates the fallen in World War II. It was carved by the famous Robert Thompson of Kilburn and like all his work, has his trade mark – a mouse – on the door too.

There is usually an attendant in the church from whom one can obtain the key to open a door through which is a spiral stone staircase leading to a museum which contains a great variety of the town's one-time features, including a set of stocks in surprisingly good condition. When one descends into the body of the church and closes the door, one must look up to the corner of the wall adjacent to the doorway and there in carved stone is the Beverley Imp. So Lincoln is not the only possessor of an Imp! There are surprises at every turn in this wonderful church which justify many hours of exploration. A pair of opera glasses or binoculars will help to see the fine detail of the bosses on the ceiling of the nave.

Before visiting the Minster we might well pause for lunch. Whilst sitting in an old inn in the corner of the Saturday Market one may notice a surprisingly large number of tall and fair men who come in for a drink and food. Tall and fair? Surely they are descendants of the Scandinavians who, even before the Conquest, and after, came over and settled hereabouts. Maybe the proportion of such men is diminishing as Beverley has now become a place to live not only in retirement but from which to commute to Hull and return in the evening.

On our way to visit the Minster – the Parish Church! – along pedestrianised streets, we must stop in Register Street and visit the Guildhall. It stands inconspicuously and can easily be missed. Four rather severe looking columns support the pediment, and inside, apart from the Information Centre, is a very attractive former court room which dates back some 230 years. The ceiling of this is a wonderful work in the art of plastering, the main motif is the figure of Justice, but for once she is not blindfold. This, like all the ceiling work, is of pale blue and white in keeping with the colours of Beverley's armorial bearings. At the rear of the Court is the original wall of the fourteenth century timber framing of the house which was used as a town hall until 1762 when the hall was rebuilt at that time. This priceless section of the wall was apparently just covered up to fit in with the new look! More recent repairs and renewals revealed it and it extends upwards to the kitchen quarters. On the ground floor is a realistic Victorian type of office with two lifelike models of clerks, one at a high desk and one at a low. The typewriter although ancient is perhaps a little too modern to fit in with the period enacted.

Upstairs is the Mayor's parlour, a beautiful room, but only open on Wednesdays and Bank Holidays. On the walls are photographs and copies of portraits of the mayors of Beverley since 1573. Among them are famous names such as Wilberforce. Then there is the Magistrates' room with much pewter tableware; also another room with sketches of the three of the town's Bars which were demolished. If you were wondering what the other three were like when passing through North Bar, here is the chance to see.

The Minster can be approached from either Eastgate or Highgate. The latter is perhaps a better approach because of the view from it of the north tower of the Minster, besides which there are quite unique places of refreshment on the left hand side. The Monks Walk and the . . .and Albert for instance. If you are neither hungry nor thirsty nor have the time to browse among attractive pottery displays, then make straight down the street and into the north porch of the Minster. Beverley Minster, a masterpiece of architecture seems to have arisen from the Monastery of St. John (of Beverley) who left the Bishopric of York to spend his retirement here in 718. Eventually it became a sanctuary. Pilgrims, thieves and rogues sought Beverley and sank on their knees in thankfulness when they came in sight of the place. Inside is a large chair carved out of stone – the Freed Stool. On reaching it, the fugitive was safe, such was the magic of St. John. This magic is further evidenced by the fact that the redoubtable William I in his ravaging of the North, left Beverley alone as he did not want to disturb the peace of St. John and his works. The latter was one of the four saints of the North of England, St. Peter of York, St. Cuthbert of Durham and St. Wilfred of Ripon. The Minster occupies the site where the town began to develop as it was near the river Hull and the Beverley Beck, with access to the sea. Eventually ship building became one of the town's industries, but little is done in that line of business today.

The great nave is apt to fill one with awe and makes one realize how much faith men had to spend their lives, generation after generation, building this wonderful evidence of it, stone by precious stone, each one painstakingly shaped and carved with pride before they saw it in place to remain there for ever and a day to the Glory of God. To kneel down and say a prayer seems to be the only thing to do ... for the moment. Then obtain a guide or a guide book and look for the countless treasures – they are not hard to find and admire.

Outside, in an extensive meadow to the south, one can obtain the one and only full view of the Minster, and what a view of that great church, which incidentally, is largely constructed from limestone from as far away as Tadcaster. Hence the pearly white appearance.

Round by the East Window is a busy little street and at the T Junction is the sixteenth century Sun Inn, one of the few remaining half-timbered houses in the town. We turn left and after a right turn the Friary comes into view, as well as the railway and good signs of industry to prove that Beverley is not becoming just a Georgian museum with a long history behind it. The Georgian period was something of a Golden Age when prosperity here enabled a splendid programme of building and rebuilding handsome properties which enhance the town today and make it a lovely place to walk and live in, this 'BEVERLAC', the old name derived from the haunt of the Beaver. Hence the Beaver of the armorial bearings.

The Friary and its garden have survived the spread of industry, but perhaps not quite because some of the foundations to the east of it are now under the railway track. Here it is then, with its ancient stones in the shadow of the Minster, open to the public as a Youth Hostel, a rare survival of the Middle Ages when the Blackfriars came here and established themselves. The Friary Trust undertook restoration. One priceless piece of workmanship has been re-erected in the garden. It is a fifteenth century doorway into the original Guildhall. Here again Tadcaster limestone appears to be in evidence, and at its side in the mellow brick-work is a little story on a plaque telling one how the lovely arched doorway came to be erected there.

As we take our leave of Beverley, the picture postcard villages of Cherry Burton, Bishop Burton, Swanland and Welton point a welcoming finger which we should not resist for they well repay a visit, and of course Beverley is their main shopping centre, especially on Wednesday or Saturday.

Knaresborough

Whitby, ancient and modern

Conisbrough Castle

Richmond from the Castle Keep

KNARESBOROUGH

A band of magnesian limestone stretches from the River Tees in the north to the Don in the south in the County of York. In places there are quite wide gaps, especially in the north. In the south, there are some which are very narrow indeed. The main rivers, the Swale, Ure, Nidd, Wharfe, Aire (and Calder) and the Don either cut through it or find gaps in it in their efforts to reach the sea via the Humber – that great waterway used by invaders from Scandinavia and indeed Rome to colonise vast areas in Yorkshire and the north midland counties.

One of the most if not *the* most, spectacular cuttings through this band of limestone must surely be by the River Nidd at Knaresborough. Curiously enough the Nidd which, apart from its infant days when it passes a romantic course through an area of caves and potholes, is a quiet and shy river, hidden from view for the most part as it pursues its serpentine way to the Ouse at Nun Monkton. Just past the village of Ripley, however, it enters the magnesian belt and after a spectacular horse-shoe bend and minor rapids, it arrives at Knaresborough, or rather at the foot of the cliff on the top of which the greater part of the town stands.

The visitor to Knaresborough soon finds himself at the substantial remains (though scattered) of the one-time Norman stronghold, the castle, on the very edge of the ravine from where you can enjoy the much photographed and painted view. A good way of entering the town is by the railway which crosses the ravine by means of an attractive viaduct with the river far below; it matters not which side of the railway carriage one is sitting, the view is quite outstanding. The town proudly stands mainly on the highest point, but straggles down to the river upstream from the viaduct. There are several ways down to Waterside, but one in particular is called Water Bag Bank, an ancient cobbled way used by carriers of water in leather bags for the use of the folk in town.

At the foot of the bank is Manor Cottage, the one remaining thatched dwelling in Knaresborough. Opposite is the old Manor House with a Georgian exterior but containing an interior of a much earlier age. A decade or so ago it was, for a time, a café and restaurant. Here one is spoiled for choice. To the left is a long but very interesting little road which leads along the foot of the cliff to the House in the Rock and the Chapel of Our Lady often referred to in error as St. Robert's Chapel, both are carved out of the living rock and faced up, and finally to St. Robert's Cave which lies between the road and the river. The alternative is to turn right and reach the High Bridge over the Nidd, passing on the way the punt and rowing boat moorings.

At the bridge, we cross the highway and enter Conyngham Hall Park riverside walk. The Hall, in which the late Sir Harold Mackintosh of toffee fame lived from 1924 to 1942, has been occupied by a number of institutions as headquarters. It has a grand looking facade with four columns supporting a huge pediment.

The Chapel of Our Lady

The immediate grounds are kept in beautiful condition by the local council which owns the property.

Leaving the Hall, we return to the riverside path upstream and presently come to a wide footbridge, and crossing this an enormous flat field appears before us. It is shaped like a horse-shoe round which the river makes its way with a path at its side. One tends to linger here and admire the sylvan beauty of it all, especially the opposite bank which is very steep and clothed with a great variety of trees some of which are very tall. A little more than halfway round the horse-shoe bend one can follow a path which eventually rises very, very steeply, but let us be content and return to the riverside path, this time on the opposite side of the water from Conyngham Hall. After a while, there is a signpost bearing the legend 'Conyngham Hall Trail' on our right. If we follow this up a path at the side of a stream coming down a steep sided little valley, crammed with trees and wild flowers of all descriptions, after passing an enormous willow tree of great age and which has seen better days, we reach two bridges which lead to a variety of charming walks.

Back on the High Bridge, we can make our way to Scotton, a nearby village, once the home of the notorious Yorkshireman, Guy Fawkes, a zealous Catholic, who was caught in the act, on the eve of 5th. November 1605, of preparing to ignite the gunpowder previously placed in the vaults of the House of Lords. However, if the spirit moves, we can visit the home of that one-time fabulous lady, Mother Shipton, a dark and gloomy cave in the hillside. Prophecies galore are attributed to her, especially the verse which included the words:

> "Carriages without horses will go
> . . .
> And accidents will fill the world with woe"

These words and many others were, it is stated on good authority, fabricated by a Brighton bookseller, many years after Mother Shipton's days. However, it can be conveniently fitting to let our imagination run riot when we view the cave and visualise Mother Shipton sitting at a stone table with parchment and a quill pen using who knows what for ink!

Back to reality, we now move on to the famous Dropping Well and see that in a relatively short time a pair of socks or some knitting can be turned to stone through the action of lime charged water which falls over a large overhanging rock onto the odd things which have been hung there.

Henry VIII's famous antiquary, John Leland, came to Knaresborough and even he was intrigued with the Dropping Well, but not with Mother Shipton to whom he makes no reference whatever. Here is what he says about the Well:

> "a well of a wonderful nature, caullid Dropping welle.
> For out of the great rokkes by it distillith water
> continually into it. This water is so could and of

such nature, that what thing so ever . . .ys caste in,
or growith about the rokke and in touchid of this
water, growith ynto stone."

A short walk from the Well brings us to The Dropping Well Inn and the Low
Bridge across which and to the right we soon see on our left the House in the
Rock, the top of which is almost level with the limestone cliff's summit. Almost
alongside is the Chapel of Our Lady of the Crag. Both are carved out of the
living rock and approached by a very steep path from the road; the former consists
of four floors which are faced up with stone with one window on each. At one
time you could enter at the basement, for a small fee, and proceed up the several
flights of stairs to the top. At the time of writing the house is uninhabited as it
is regarded as unsafe. It is owned by the authorities of Ampleforth College and
efforts are being made to restore it – a quite unique dwelling.

The Chapel of Our Lady of the Crag (often called St. Robert's Chapel in error)
is approached in much the same way as the House in the Rock, faced up with
stone, an ancient door and leaded window. Inside there is little seating but the
altar is colourfully adorned. Carved on the right of the door, perhaps guarding
it, is a figure carrying a sword believed to represent a Knight Templar (not St
Robert!) To see real evidence of St. Robert, we must descend to the Abbey Road,
turn left and pass several attractive fairly modern houses and eventually turning
a corner come to the site of the Priory of the Trinitarians founded in A.D.1287.
Little is left of the buildings, but the gable end of a barn abutting the road bears
a plaque reciting briefly the story of the priory. The monks ventured into the
towns and countryside begging alms for the poor of Knaresborough, money to
pay the ransom of Christian hostages held by the Saracens in the Holy Land
during the Crusades, and also to help in the upkeep of their Priory. In this
connection, we must not forget that an important section of the Knight Templars
was at near at hand Ribston. More shades of the Crusades.

Leaving Priory Farm and Priory Cottage in their delightful setting, we persist
a little longer on that little road, and suddenly we see a glazed plaque on the
right – St. Robert's Cave! A steep descent by means of a series of shored up
steps leads us to a little plateau on which still lie the foundations of a chapel
and then on the right is the entrance to the cave. St. Robert, born in York, *c* 1160
of a good family – his father was a mayor of that city – chose to lead the life
of an ascetic in poverty and prayer. He was never canonised but through his
selfless efforts and good works he came to be known as St. Robert. King John
of Magna Carta fame who had heard of St. Robert's extraordinary life and the
powers which went with it was so impressed that he visited Knaresborough to
see him. Not only did he see him in prayer, but waited until the prayer was
finished before he spoke to him. As a result of the interview, King John granted

him land amounting to about 40 acres in that area. There is still plenty of meadow and pasture land in the area between the Priory and the Cave, and passing it, one finds oneself lost in wonder at the sheer dedication of the man. He was never alone because he said he had always three companions with him, The Father, Son and Holy Ghost. Eventually one reaches once again the site of the Trinitarian priory established a short time after St. Robert's death. The latter's lands were then given to the Trinitarians.

We make haste along Abbey Road and Waterside to the High Bridge and join the main road from Harrogate into the town. At first the road is called Bond End.

On the way up and after turning to the right into the High Street, we reach a beautiful mansion on our right. This is Knaresborough House which now houses the Council Offices. It has a great history going back to c.1768 and was the home of a well thought of family of the name of Collins and occupied later by Knaresborough's longest serving vicar, Revd. Thomas Collins, who was the incumbent for over 60 years. The house is situated in attractive grounds and open to the public.

Further up the High Street are two special buildings on the left; the first is the Old School House perched up on high ground on which is a large plaque which bears the following legend:

"This School was endowed by the late Thos. Richardfon Efq. in the year 1765 with this Houfe (and by his will in 1775) with the sum of Money with which an Eftate 45L. per annum situate in Follifoot was purchafed by the Truftees appointed in and by the Deed of Endowment.

The land tax of the Eftate which amounted to 1L.6s. per annum was redeemed by a Subfcription of Several Inhabitants of Knarefborough."

BENEFACTIONS TO THE SCHOOL

		L.	*s.*	*d.*
1770	Danfon Roundell Efq.	42	–	–
14th. Apl. 1795	Mr. Jno. Simpfon Highftreet	10	–	–
26th. May 1803	Mrs. Ann Shatwell	21	–	–
1ft. July 1803	Mr. Chriftopher Walton	20	–	–
13th. July 1803	Mr. James Collins	100	–	–
30th. May 1804	Mr. John Walton	100	–	–
	and by will	200	–	–
5th. June 1804	Mr. Michael Broadbelt	10	10	–
	Mrs. Ann Broadbelt	25	–	–
4th. Sept. 1808	and by Will per Annum (Not paid now)	10	–	–

31 Dec.	Mrs. Shepherd	200	–	–
14 Jan. 1809	Mrs. Henry Hopps	10	–	–
21st. Aug. 1810	John Watson Esq. by Will	50	–	–
4th. Dec. 1820	Mrs. Elizth Collins by D:	100	–	–
9th. Oct. 1826	The late Mr. Walsh	50	–	–
26th.March 1842	Mr. W. Catton	10	–	–

N.B. It is interesting to note that the Roundell family lived in the Knaresborough district as far back as the fifteenth century, and that many years later the Richardson family became related to them.

The Roundells of Scriven were invariably baptised in Knaresborough Parish Church; they bought Gledstone House, Marton, near Skipton which became the seat of a Revd. Danson Richardson Roundell who still held land at Thruscross in the Forest of Knaresborough.

The Revd. Danson Roundell (like his forbears) did not forget his connection with Thruscross because he donated a plot of land in the 1870s for the creation of a new churchyard at West End – at the head of the Washburn valley – and cash of £14 when it was decided to rebuild the old church there. Alas, nearly 100 years later (1966) the land and indeed the church were drowned in the waters of Thruscross reservoir.

The second building is Cromwell House, a little higher up the street. It is reliably stated that the redoubtable man himself stayed here soon after the siege by the Roundheads. Although the house was rebuilt in the eighteenth century, the room in which Cromwell slept is still there. There is a story that the daughter of the house had the job of taking the warming pan to air Cromwell's bed and when she saw him, he was sitting there untying his garters. The girl goes on to say: "Having aired the bed, I went out and shutting the door after me, stopped and peeped through the keyhole when I saw him rise from his feet, advance to the bed and fall on his knees, in which attitude I left him for some time. When I returned again, I found him still at prayer, and this was his custom every night so long as he stayed at our house; from which I concluded he must be a good man, and this opinion I always maintained afterwards though I heard him very much blamed and exceedingly abused".

We cannot blame Cromwell for destroying the great Royal stronghold, the castle, because, no doubt, he would have been proud of his men having captured it more or less whole. A few years later, Parliament ordered the destruction of so many castles in Yorkshire, including Knaresborough and indeed that great bastion, Pontefract, so let us go and have a look at the once great castle and the well chosen site on which it is built, but on our way the church demands our attention.

Here we leave the High Street and visit the famous church down Vicarage Lane. And what a church! It lies in a very spacious area in the middle of the old Manor of Beechill and is dedicated to St. John the Baptist. Established in A.D.1117, it became the property of Nostell Priory, Wakefield and later of the Archbishop Grey of York. It is, of course, Knaresborough Parish Church and packed with interest. Though it has been rebuilt and amended many times since 1117 traces of the original building can be seen in the chancel, in the blocked up windows each side of the East Window and in the string course.

The parish registers date from 1561 and contain records of Baptisms of the children of famous characters – Eugene Aram, Daniel Clark and Richard Houseman. Eugene Aram was a Knaresborough schoolmaster and found guilty of murdering Clark, Houseman being implicated but not found guilty. The skeleton of a body considered to be that of Clark was discovered, some 14 years after he had 'disappeared' from Knaresborough, found by a workman digging for limestone near the town.

The story goes that Clark had obtained a number of valuable items on credit and at the same time Aram began to pay his outstanding bills. They had both been seen in the company of Houseman a short time before Aram got another schoolmaster's job as far away as Kings Lynn, Norfolk, and Clark had 'disappeared'. On the discovery of the skeleton in 1758, Houseman became suspect, but told the court that he had actually seen Aram strike down Clark in St. Robert's Cave. On discovery of a skeleton in the cave as a result of Houseman's statement, Aram was brought back to Knaresborough, imprisoned at York and a year later hanged. What happened as regards the skeleton found by the workman? Houseman said it wasn't Clark's. Whose was it?

Of all the treasures in the church, the Slingsby Chapel must surely demand our interest. It contains the tombs and murals of a family which held sway for several centuries in the Knaresborough area. During the Civil War, Sir Henry Slingsby, a Royalist, was beheaded in the Tower of London in 1658; a black marble slab in the chapel covers his grave. An altar tomb of Sir Charles Slingsby marks the last of the direct male line of that famous family in 1869.

An interesting incident in the life of William Slingsby occurred when he was hunting: he discovered in the late sixteenth century a well of springing water which tasted like some of the mineral waters found in watering places on the continent. He had the area round the well paved and it became known as Tewit Well. This was about three miles from Knaresborough when Harrogate consisted only of a few cottages and a farmhouse or two, so the former could claim that it converted 'a bleak and dreary heath' into the Stray and subsequently the fashionable watering place as more and more healing waters were found.

As we leave the church, and have a look at the outside, we notice the clock on the tower which figures on so many postcards of Knaresborough. Above the face are the words:

Redeeming the Time

It makes us all think that we should make the best of the precious little time we have on earth for the common good, as well as examining ourselves to make sure that in the end we are fit to enter whatever God intended for us.

Walking up Kirkgate, we may cross the railway line or go under the subway according to the circumstances, and eventually reach the Market Place, always busy whether market day or not. The 'must' here is surely 'Ye Oldest Chymist Shoppe'. Established in the Reign of George I, 1720, it is the oldest chemist's shop in England. There it stands on even older foundations, mature red brick gables very well maintained, inviting customers into the low interior with its oak beams and very much to catch the eye. Its contents vary from modern camera films to ancient remedies, not forgetting the lavender water for which it is famous, one could almost say the world over. An ornate jar with perforated lid is still in evidence, a reminder of the days when leeches were kept in it and used for blood letting. The name of the contents of the jar is plain to be seen on the outside just in case one wondered! A charming girl dressed in the apparel of a long past period may well be pleased to serve you with any item of your choice.

As we stand once again among the ruins of the castle, we wonder what stood there before the Normans ravaged the North and eventually built it up again. It seems obvious that long before 1066, Knaresborough's vantage point would have been discovered, even before Saxon times, and developed as an important centre.

The oldest chemist's shop in England

Judging by the 'Knaresborough Hoard' of bronze vessels and other artifacts now in York Museum, the Romans did not overlook the place. Evidence of an earlier age has also been found in nearby Scotton perched on top of the limestone ridge a little upstream.

In the Domesday Book it is spelled Chenaresburgh, as one would expect, as the Normans did not use the English letter 'K'. Even now, the French rarely use it except in the spelling of kilo. In less than 100 years, the Norman castle was built, in full swing and a great centre – one of the chief military and financial areas of the north. Later King John came to Knaresborough and stayed at the castle on several occasions. Apart from his visit to St. Robert, it appears that the very first Royal Maundy Thursday in England was held at Knaresborough by the King himself in A.D. 1210, when money and clothing were given to the poor. A notable event, indeed, in the little town of Knaresborough.

During the summer there are guided tours of the castle which include the interior, and what an interior! The dungeon with one tiny window is an awe-inspiring place with a central pillar and vaulted roof. It is like standing under an enormous mushroom with stone walls some fifteen feet thick around you. Builders of modern prisons should note, especially if they don't want prisoners to escape.

Across the greensward and flower beds is the Old Courthouse, now a museum full of fascinating effects. Shades of the many characters of the town's past, especially Blind Jack Metcalf. Blind Jack was a most unusual character. At the age of six in 1723, he had smallpox and as a result lost the sight of both eyes. He must have been given second sight because he soon found his way around with great determination and energy, learned to play the fiddle, and even acted as guide to travellers, especially at night and in the misty weather. He traded in many things – horses for instance, and even ran a stage coach between Knaresborough and Harrogate. He once walked from London to Knaresborough only to find on his return that his beloved girl friend had become engaged to someone else. A true romantic, he sought her out immediately. She fell into his arms and they eloped and got married, had a family and lived together for 40 years; he survived until his 93rd. year. In his latter years, he took to road building and made his name by putting layers of heather and covering them with gravel especially over soft or boggy land, not only near at hand but in many other parts of the north. He used his famous staff for measuring depths and a viameter for distances. The viameter can be seen in the museum.

As we stand once again and have a last look at the famous view from the Castle grounds, we are reminded of the ancient Forest of Knaresborough. What area did it cover? In the north-west it included Padside and its ruined Hall, Thornthwaite, Darley and Menwith, Birstwith and Felliscliffe, Clifton, Fewston, Haverah Park with its John O'Gaunt's castle ruin, Norwood, Clint, Ripley, Hampsthwaite, Killinghall and, of course, Knaresborough itself with Scriven and Scruton.

The word Forest, in the Middle Ages, meant an administrative area, a hunting area subject to rules and regulations, far from being an enormous forest of trees. Of course, there were many areas of woodland as well as cultivated fields. It was formed between Domesday and A.D.1167. An interesting series of boundary stones can still be seen downstream from the superb little pack-horse bridge over Red Beck at Thornthwaite. The title deeds relating to parcels of land in the forest make interesting reading.

Many famous names come to mind, too:

Mother Shipton, Guy Fawkes, Blind Jack Metcalf, St. Robert, King John, Cromwell, Roundell, Richardson, Slingsby, Collins, Eugene Aram . . .one could go on, but we must not forget Lord Inman. A plaque at the top of Water Bag Bank bears the legend:

PHILIP, LORD INMAN OF KNARESBOROUGH
1892 – 1979

On this site was born Lord Inman of Knaresborough.
    A man who, from humble beginnings rose to be
Chairman of Charing Cross Hospital, Chairman of the
B.B.C. and Lord Privy Seal, whilst maintaining a
life-long affection for the town of his birth

    Erected by
        Knaresborough Historical Society 1980

HELMSLEY

What an abundance of glorious walks there are to be had in and around this ancient market town. In the late spring on a sunny day on Duncombe Park Terrace, as wide as a cricket pitch, milk white with daisies, God is truly in His Heaven. One can stroll from a domed temple at one end to a domed temple at the other, a distance of about one third of a mile. On one side it is wooded with a gap to enable one to stop and admire the house, and on the other is a very steep wooded slope down to the meandering river Rye.

But wait, let us explore the town itself. On entering Helmsley from any direction, one is immediately struck with its unique atmosphere. On the one hand there is, in the market place, a statue of the 2nd.Lord Feversham; ancient hostelries and buildings overlook him from all sides. On the other hand, the modern motorist is seen parking his car, paying and displaying, and then consulting the menus displayed at the entrances of places to eat and drink.

How many venture forth and enter Buckingham Square, just round the corner then park their car at the foot of the castle? Not a large proportion. Maybe it is because it is only the remains of the east tower which are visible from the market place, but if one takes the trouble to see it at close quarters, one is quite astounded. The whole of the castle perched on the top of the steep grass covered ramparts comes into view, but on mounting the steps, one finds that there is not just one ditch going right round the castle but two for added protection. In places, one can see where the solid limestone has been cut away to enable the inner ditch to be complete.

The gatehouse is flanked by two drum towers still standing as they did hundreds of years ago on the edge of the limestone base. Today, a wooden bridge enables the visitor to cross the outer ditch from the south barbican to the south gatehouse and again to the main part of the castle.

Once 'inside', the extent is surprisingly large. All that remains of the east wall of the tower are its foundations. The way that the west side still stands right to the top shows how well it was built before the Civil War brought about the castle's downfall.

The views from the castle are far reaching. Near at hand, the Victorian top of the church tower just peeps over what remains of the north wall. As one walks towards the latter only the roof tops and chimneys appear.

The castle was built in the twelfth century on land in the centre of an estate granted by the redoubtable William I to Robert de Mortain, a relative of the conqueror, but William II saw things differently and in 1088 confiscated Mortain's estate. However, in 1120 Walter Espec became the owner – he was a soldier and played an important part on the occasion of the Battle of the Standard 1138 (see stone memorial on the A167, a little north of Northallerton).

As well as Rievaulx Abbey, he founded several other monastic houses, but

The East Tower of Helmsley Castle, high above the town

had no direct heir and the estate passed to his brother-in-law, Peter de Roos. The latter's descendants held the estate with the exception of about 23 years until 1508 when it became the property of the Manners family. Then came the Civil War.

A surprising feature of Helmsley Castle is the Tudor Mansion built within the confines of the building – it was considered to be more comfortable than the existing domestic quarters. Entrance to this is by means of two stone staircases, one is in the tower and one at the opposite end. It was upsetting to see several sections of stone mullions filled in with brick. It would be rather nice to see these windows brought into line with the others with small leaded panes. Perhaps there would be no need for them to be glazed with Flemish glass!

Inside, the author was delighted to see and admire an exhibition of water-colour paintings by Girtin and also by Cotman and Turner. Then there is another room with a unique fireplace, decorated plaster ceiling and frieze. The walls were oak-panelled. Everything is in good condition considering the circumstances. There are basements to explore, too.

Helmsley Castle, apart from a feeble incursion by the Scots, had no battles to face for something like 400 years. However, it was no match during the Civil War against the Parliamentary forces under Fairfax in 1644 when it lost its one and only encounter of note. Even then it lost honourably – the men were allowed to march out with their small arms.

Rather like the end of the Wars of the Roses, when Henry VII married Elizabeth, daughter of Edward IV who was of the House of York, the second Duke of Buckingham married Thos. Fairfax's daughter, Mary. The Civil War came to an end in 1659.

One can sit on a sun-warmed stone and let the imagination run riot, soaking in the atmosphere of the place and be intrigued with the beautiful parkland to the west which promises great interest. Duncombe Park, in fact. Let us then complete our brief tour of the castle by crossing the ditches to the north by means of the modern wooden bridge and make our way back to the town.

At the top left of the market place is the ancient half-timbered Rectory House, now part of the Black Swan Hotel, which contains some fine internal timbering. Part of the Feathers Hotel on our right is Thorpe's cottage, a fifteenth century building. Here one can enjoy victuals in warmth and comfort – black beams abounding. Another half-timbered house is in Castlegate (back of the Town Hall). This is said to be sixteenth century and is called The Manor House, or Gatehouse. In Castlegate is a working blacksmith who will make you flat-sided baskets to hang on your wall and fill with plants.

At the low end of the town, the river Rye is crossed by a bridge consisting of two parts – one is ancient and the other modern, but they are integrated into one with a single carriageway. Look over the parapet on the downstream side and you will see two ancient pointed arches, on the upstream side the arches are rounded. The inquisitive visitor will cross the bridge and descend to the river

Helmsley

bank, look under the bridge and find the dividing line between the ancient and modern is plain to be seen, which suggests that the original bridge would only allow one-way traffic. Even now, there is no room for side-walks.

Before leaving for the town centre again, a walk along Ryegate is well worthwhile. No.22, a Georgian cottage, has mortared into the south wall, the Arms of the Overton family, prominent burgesses in the fourteenth and fifteenth centuries. One wonders if it came from the church of All Saints in the town.

Back in the town, we go through the church gates and enter the building itself through an elaborate Norman arch – one of the few remaining very old remains of what originally stood there. What a pity so much of the church has been Victorianized! Even so, there is much to appreciate. The Chancel arch, for example, has the original arch of four orders, like the entrance porch.

The Baptistry is sometimes overlooked in an ancient church such as this as one instinctively looks towards the east window first of all. Attracting attention as one approaches the chancel are the carvings on the arch – the outer ring consists of a set of hoodmasks with large eyes, moustaches and outstuck tongues. The inner ring is decorated with a chain of carved beads, the next consists of carved chevrons, whilst the third is quite plain.

Columba Chapel is a must, as the murals and glass show the coming of Christianity to the north of England. There are scenes, in the south wall window, from the life of St Columba, who being banished from Ireland for murder, brought Christianity to Scotland and founded the monastery of Iona. The crucifix in the Chapel was brought from no less a place than Oberammergau by the famous Revd. Charles Norris Gray who came to Helmsley in 1870 – he was the son of the Bishop of Cape Town. Not only was he a good boxer, but a real go-getter and certainly put Helmsley on the map, both ecclesiastically and secularly.

To the right on our way out is the Baptistry. On the floor is the tomb of the 10th. Lord (Thomas) de Roos with brass effigies of himself and his wife, now well worn it is feared. Then there is a picture of the church before rebuilding. There is also a glass case containing many relics including a yoke from a slave in Africa, and a letter from Dr. Livingstone to Mrs. Gray, wife of the famous vicar.

Entrance from the east to Duncombe Park starts immediately in Buckingham Square approached from Castlegate. It is a mile drive through the parkland to the House. About half-way there is a pay booth where you obtain tickets for House and Gardens or Gardens only. Nearby is an immaculate car park and a Visitors Centre and café (just as immaculate) through which you pass to the House, at first hidden by trees. Then it all stands before you – grand entrance gates and steps to the main door. In a very impressive and lofty hall you show your tickets and are received gracefully. You learn that the second Earl of Feversham was killed on the Somme in 1916 and his family had to pay very heavy death duties. He gave his life for King and Country and the family had to pay for it. Subsequent to this, the property was let to a girls' school and it was not until 1985 that the Feversham family were able to resume residence in part of the House, much of which is open to visitors.

Beautiful English and Continental furniture and pictures can be seen on the ground floor. In one of the bedrooms, the bed is somewhat higher than most and a short flight of wooden steps placed alongside enables one to get between the sheets with ease. If one of the guides is around, she will lift the top step which will bring forth not only a smile but a commode! En suite!!

The original house was designed in 1713 by one William Wakefield for the Duncombe family from whom the Fevershams are descended. It suffered three separate fires, the last in 1985 when it was rebuilt in the original style. The gardens are very extensive and, of course, include the terrace previously mentioned.

Before we leave Helmsley, a visit to Rievaulx Terrace is a must. We leave the town by means of the road leading to Rievaulx Abbey, but at the crest, we come to the entrance to the famous terrace, where Sir Thomas Duncombe decided to build a Greek temple. It is now cared for by the National Trust. Inside, it is beautifully furnished but the ceiling at once attracts one's attention. It consists of a series of paintings by Borgnis, an Italian artist, showing mythological scenes with plump goddesses. His great ability and the very high quality of paint he used is quite apparent in scenes portraying Vulcan and Venus, Pan and Cupid, Diana and Endymion as well as many others. It is said that he spent something like three years on his back doing this work. At the other end of the terrace is an unfurnished Tuscan Temple. It stands there quite serene in its lovely setting. On our way there far down below, near the river, we get glimpses of that silver grey abbey of Rievaulx. Unfortunately we cannot scramble our way down to it, but return to the road and descend that way.

Pass under those lovely arches of stone, each one drenched in centuries of sunshine and rainstorm, still standing there to the Glory of God and proof of the utter dedication of those men who carefully placed each stone in position to say nothing of those who carved them. Time would not matter so long as each stone received devout attention.

Founded by Walter Espec c.1160 it held sway and influence over a very wide area for 400 years until, like so many other monastic houses, Henry VIII considered they held too much power.

This Cistercian abbey has an exhibition centre in which the visitor can see how the Abbot and his men and those following them developed their business. Mind you, they were given land and property. Nevertheless, they made good use of it and prospered. What a great legacy and tourist attraction has resulted, together with its delightful situation in the lovely valley of the Rye and nearby village.

WHITBY

Whales, all manner of fish, Captain Cook, William Scoresby, St. Hilda, floating dock, jet, ancient inns, cobbles and keel boats, Khyber Pass, Swing Bridge, Count Dracula, holiday makers. One could go on and on . . .

A famous picture postcard view of Whitby from the top of the Khyber Pass on the west cliff shows much of the town and, across the water in the harbour, the ancient church of St. Mary and the Abbey ruins of St. Hilda; a lovely prospect of Whitby.

Just to digress a little, let us, after visiting the Tower of London, walk along Wapping High Street for ten minutes or so and visit the Prospect of Whitby. It may seem a long ten minutes, but a building on the right named St Hilda's Wharf assures us that the Prospect of Whitby cannot be far away, for just round the corner there it stands. It is the oldest inn on the banks of the Thames and dates from 1520 and was originally known as the Devil's Tavern. Some years later (c.1777), it was renamed The Prospect of Whitby, because colliers from the north of England brought coal to the wharves at Wapping, and one special ship called *The Prospect* was built at Whitby. The inn is a curious mixture of the old and the new. Downstairs one can eat and drink at tables immediately overlooking the water in an olde worlde atmosphere, whilst upstairs is an elegant restaurant, again with views from a balcony overlooking the Thames. The inn was frequented by Charles Dickens and Samuel Pepys. From the balconies are wide views including the site of the Execution Dock across the river where pirates were hanged in chains until three tides had washed over them. Now the view includes the famous Canary Wharf building. Today, as at Whitby itself, sea-faring vessels are not so common as they were hereabouts, but close your eyes and bear in mind the hanging inn sign showing *The Prospect* in full sail and it is easy to imagine what the river traffic looked like some 200 years ago. Associations with Yorkshire such as this are not rare, but let us have a close look at Whitby itself and the men and women whose lives were bound up with its history in one way or another.

Whitby is a striking place – it doesn't just nestle at the foot of the cliffs which rise steeply from the harbour from which the river Esk joins the North Sea, but climbs them. One hundred and ninety-nine wide steps lead one up to the church and the abbey on the east side, whilst the Khyber Pass or indeed Flowergate, lead one steeply to Georgian houses, and then to Victorian and Edwardian houses and hotels which came about with the entry into the town of George Hudson's railway down the Esk valley. This development on the west cliff brought the holiday makers, especially as far down below is a glorious wide stretch of golden sand.

Whilst we have plenty of energy let us find our way to the Swing Bridge which joins the east and west banks of the river (and indeed the harbour) at its

The Captain Cook Memorial on the West Cliff, Whitby

narrowest part; we cross it and hurry along to our left on Church Street – there are many attractions on the way – and reach the 'Church Stairs'. Alongside the stairs is a cobbled road, very, very steep, called the Donkey Road. On the way up, too, we see very many houses and cottages with red pantiled roofs. It is easy to stop and think of the many generations of sea-faring men and their families who have spent their lives there, every man, woman and child connected with the sea in one way or another.

At the top, the church first commands our attention – it must be one of the most remarkable of its kind. The great urge is to go inside before taking a close look at the exterior. It seems as if a group of ship builders of old had raised it, as one is reminded of the interior of the hull of a ship. Even the gallery, joining the north and south galleries looks like a bridge which it is, in fact. Its great length is most noticeable and it is said that it was as long as this in the twelfth century when it was first built. In spite of the Norman influence, the late Georgian additions which are quite apparent fit in well with the rest of the building. The old box pews are there in abundance and the three-decker pulpit is so placed that the preacher can see every part of the church – transept and choir – there is no hiding place!

One of the outstanding features of the church's exterior is the massive tower which seems to have been built to withstand all the gales and storms that have ever swept over that historic cliff top or are ever likely to do so in the future.

A noticeable feature is the absence of stained glass, except, of course, the East Window. Puritan influence?

In the churchyard are countless tombstones which bear the names of daring seafaring men of Whitby. Alas, some of them have long since shown signs of severe weathering and worn so thin in places that many of the inscriptions are illegible. There is one very tall obelisk at the entrance to the yard, erected not so many ages ago. It is most attractively carved on all four sides and is in memory of a lay brother who significantly added to our country's Christian literature and true object of life. To learn a little more of his life we make our way a little further up the hill to the Abbey of St. Hilda.

Like Lindisfarne, Whitby Abbey reminds us of the antiquity of the site; here in the seventh century, before the present building was erected, St. Hilda swayed northern Christendom and Caedmon wrote his songs. Like Lindisfarne stones, those at Whitby have been pitted and grooved by salt laden winds and rain. In addition they suffered from naval bombardment during the First World War. Perhaps one of the most enduring meetings held there was that which made the decision to finally fix the dates when Easter should be held. St. Hilda presided at that meeting, the Synod of Whitby. A.D. 664.

Though Caedmon was no youngster, he did not enjoy the 'rude alliterative' with which his fellow men passed the long nights by the fire singing songs. The story goes that one evening, he left the merry throng to tend the cattle and fell asleep. A strange voice said to him: 'Sing, Caedmon, some song to me'; in reply,

Caedmon said: 'I cannot sing and for this reason I left to tend the cattle.' The Voice said: 'Hoebeit, you shall sing to Me.' 'What then shall I sing?' and the Speaker answered him: 'The beginning of created things shalt sing.' The following morning, Caedmon recounted his story to the Abbess Hilda and she and the brethren, 'comprehending the divine grace in the man' when he had given expression to a passage of Holy Writ, bade him to assume the habit, and thereafter he sang of the creation, the fall, the history of the Jews, the redemption, and of the judgment, the pains of hell, and the joys of heaven. After Caedmon became a monk, he wrote his 'Song of Creation' and many other verses through which he became renowned.

Here then, stands this holy place, one of the most venerable in this country. It was the burial place of Saxon kings and inspired at least nine saints. Laid waste some two hundred years after the days of St. Hilda, by the Danes, it was not rebuilt until William the Conqueror's time, when it also became under the Benedictine Order. As it acquired vast estates over the years, Henry VIII did not care for it very much, so it was torn down quite violently. Originally, the abbey was the home of monks as well as nuns, each having his own little cell.

Today, the abbey is under the care of English Heritage, and there are still many evidences of the dedicated workmanship of the stone masons, especially on the western and northern sides. Facing north are two wonderful windows with exquisite tracery. Nearby there is a base of a pillar on which one can stand and take a photograph! At the official English Heritage entrance, there is the inevitable gift shop. There is also a large car park.

At the foot of the stairs to the right is Henrietta Street, up which you will find smoke issuing from little kippering businesses. One is often intrigued by the name of streets in general and in this case, one might ask, "Who was Henrietta?" She was the wife of Nathaniel Cholmley, a descendant of the family of that name who came into possession of the area way back in 1555 following the dissolution of the monasteries. There are still a few gaps between the houses, a reminder of the landslide which occurred in 1787. Further east, further landslides have taken place making progress hazardous.

Returning to the base of the 199 steps, we enter Church Street with its many shops retailing shell fish in plenty and others selling Whitby jet in its highly polished shapes and sizes. Pendants, bracelets, brooches, ornaments, beads and crosses all tempt one to buy 'just a little reminder of Whitby'. There are still one or two establishments which actually cut and polish jet on the premises.

Jet has a long history. Solinus writing in 218 specifically mentions Britain, where it is said it could be found. He called it a black jewel with little weight and that it 'burneth in water and goeth out in Oyle'. He added that when rubbed it became warm and had a magnetic quality. Maybe it was static electricity which occurred as a result of rubbing it.

Whitby jet was shipped to Scandinavia by the Vikings, and during monastic times it was used for making rosaries and crucifixes. By 1800 jet became so popular that in 1808, a factory was set up in Whitby by one John Carter and by 1873 other firms had started up and in total 1500 hands were employed cutting and polishing it in 200 workshops. There were many in Church Street where so many jet shops still exist. It became so famous in the Victorian era that a case of fine pieces was exhibited at the Great Exhibition at Crystal Palace. The deaths of the Duke of Wellington and Prince Albert contributed to the then vogue for jet ornaments and portrait busts.

Jet of such quality is rarely found anywhere else but at Whitby. Found in beds of shale it is fossilized wood of coniferous trees. The largest piece of jet ever

The Old Town Hall, Whitby

found was over six feet long and in the Museum on the west cliff many remarkable examples of the craft can be seen.

Just off Church Street is the Old Town Hall with its clock overlooking the unique little square. The date is given as MDCCLXXXVIII. At the foot of the sloping square is the old market hall. Here again Nathaniel Cholmley's influence is apparent because he built the Town Hall (and paid for it) at his side of the river! This was because his father moved the market from across the water. The Town Hall's upstairs chamber is reached by means of a spiral staircase, and in it The Court Leet was held. At one time there were stocks outside where guilty folk had to sit.

No.13 Church Street is William Scoresby House (c.1760) Whitby born William Scoresby was the inventor of the Crow's Nest on sailing ships, and a daring and skilful seaman in the northern whale fishery. His only son, also William, accompanied him on several Arctic Expeditions and at the early age of 20 was given command of the *Resolution* in place of his father. He made no less than 20 expeditions to the North West Passage, but eventually entered the church and became Vicar of Bradford. His fame was such that a Royal Research Ship – in the Antarctic this time – was named after him and some years ago appeared on a Falkland Islands postage stamp.

In the Church Street area names such as New Way Ghaut, Arguments Yard, Salt Pan Well Steps arouse one's curiosity. One old alleyway leads down to the Lifeboat building. Parallel with part of Church Street is Sandgate which is close to the water and dates from 1401, the oldest recorded street in Whitby. Its lower part was known as The Shambles and housed many butchers' shops and slaughter houses. Its proximity to the water might well suggest where unwanted offal finished up! Opposite the swing bridge end of Sandgate is another curiously named little street, Grape Lane – formerly Grope Lane as it was unlit at night. Just as it ends in a small parking place there is another famous house, The James Cook Museum. Whilst the house is furnished as it would have been in Cook's days, the pieces are reproductions, the antiques have been gathered over the years. Nevertheless it is a really worthwhile place to visit. There are several attractive rooms with views as well as many documents relating to Cook and the ships owned by Mr. John Walker, the owner of the house in which Cook lodged as a youth and indeed after he became the world famous explorer. In the attic, where Cook slept as an apprentice, there is little to see except exhibits of letters etc. Descriptive booklets and leaflets about Captain Walker and the young James and his travels are available in plenty.

"Born at Marton in Cleveland in 1728 and lost his life in Hawaii in 1779, we learn that Cook was a modest man and rather bashful; of an agreeable lively conversation, sensible and intelligent. In temper, he was somewhat hasty, but of a disposition the most friendly, benevolent and humane. His person was above six feet high, and though a good looking man, he was plain both in address and appearance. His face was full of expression, his nose extremely well shaped, his eyes which were small and of brown cast, were quick and piercing; his eyebrows prominent, which gave his countenance altogether an air of austerity!"

The words of David Samwell, Surgeon of the
famous ship *Resolution*

If we follow Church Street southwards along the waterside, we pass on our left the Seaman's Hospital, a fine building built over 300 years ago, but with a new front rebuilt some 150 years later. Further on is the floating dock where repairs to steam ships are carried out. This part of the harbour is known Abraham's Bosom, and nearby is the site of the Penny Hedge Ceremony.

Let us now return to the swing bridge and explore the west side of the town. On the way, we may be wondering: What is the Penny Hedge? A monk from Evesham is said to have been responsible for the re-establishment of the Benedictine Order when the Abbey was rebuilt. William I, William II, Henry I and Henry II duly approved of the re-establishment, but in the twelfth century, the King of Norway and others raided the place and indeed the lands around. The Abbot of Scarborough forced the insurgents to withdraw, and the monk at the time forgave them on his death bed provided they did penance. One of the penances was to erect The Penny Hedge every Ascension Eve. It consists of nine upright stakes of wood and two supporters at each end; it has to be strong enough to withstand three tides. The service of the Penny Hedge survives to this day. Why 'Penny'? One explanation seems to be that the stakes be cut by a knife of a value of one penny. Allowing for inflation, that knife would be far from cheap, even today.

Over the bridge then; to the right is the way on to the West Pier; to the left is the Railway Station and the huge car park as well as the Information Centre. However, we turn to the right and go along the West Pier where the famous Whitby haddock and other fish is landed early in the morning. Here are many fish restaurants in which one can sample their wares. There is one eating place which bears the name of a well known bird – strangely enough not one which is normally associated with the sea or sea coasts. The Transylvanian Vampire is commemorated in the Dracula Museum a little further along the pier. The vampire is said to have sailed the wintry seas and steered the ship during a violent storm into Whitby harbour. Steered by a dead man! Some years have gone by since Whitby became so newsworthy through the infamous Count, as Bram Stoker based his novel, or rather part of it, in Whitby. The Dracula Museum tells us all, and after darkness falls, we feel we ought to be on our way and leave the narrow shadowy streets if we wish to avoid fear and trembling feelings . . .

Further along the pier, we take the road up to the left and find ourselves in the Khyber Pass. This was cut through the West Cliff when the railway came to Whitby and gave access to the new development on the cliff top.

At the top of the cliff stand two striking things. The whale jaw bones and the statue of James Cook. Once again, we are reminded that the latter joined the Royal Navy as a very young man and four years later, as sailing master of the *Mercury*, he did a survey of the St. Lawrence river and the Newfoundland coast. His observations of the solar eclipse received the attention of the Royal Society and he was appointed Commander of an expedition to the Pacific, New South Wales as well as New Zealand where Mount Cook and Cook Strait, of course bear his name. On his journey southwards off the coast of North America, he eventually reached the Sandwich Islands, hitherto unknown.

Standing on that modern West Cliff and looking out to sea, one can visualise quite easily what would be in the mind of that intrepid sailor boy. The view would be much the same as now, but what lay far beyond those ever-rolling breakers must have been compelling to young James. He just had to go and see for himself.

As regards the whale bones, these were obtained by one Thor 'Dhal of Norway and Graham Leach for the town, and were erected in 1963 by the then Whitby Urban District Council.

Between the years 1753 and 1833 no less than 55 ships from Whitby were engaged in Whaling. It was an exciting and dangerous undertaking. Many men were killed, boats overturned and ships crushed in pack ice. During this period, something like 25,000 seals, 55 polar bears and 2,760 whales were brought back to Whitby, and great blubberhouses rendered oil in great quantities, much of which was in demand during the industrial revolution.

When the time drew nigh for the return of a whaling ship to Whitby, close watch was made for the sign of the masthead appearing on the horizon. If a pair of jaw bones were triced up to the mast, then the waiting wives of Whitby knew that the ship was full. Little is now left to remind one of those days, other than the pair of jaw bones standing there on the cliff top.

Back into the old part of the town, we make our way down steep Flowergate and on the right sidewalk is a very ancient set of mounting steps, so well worn that the casual passerby would easily miss them. Nearby is the famous old inn called The Little Angel. To the south and almost parallel with Flowergate is Bagdale. It has a raised pavement and one of the oldest, if not the oldest, houses in Whitby, Bagdale Hall. The son of one of the families who lived there was responsible for betraying Scarborough Castle to Cromwell . . .

And so we leave this wonderful old town and make our way westward to that fascinating former port on the river Tees, Yarm. It is wholly south of the river.

YARM

How many Yorkshiremen, especially those living in the old West Riding and even the East Riding, know exactly where it is? A few have a vague idea.

Yet, here is a quite unique and lovely town on the southern bank of the river Tees which very largely divided Yorkshire from County Durham. This old town is almost entirely enclosed in one of the many loops of that river. For the best part of 900 years it was in Yorkshire. Alas, in 1974, when changes in county boundaries took place and sometimes became a very controversial issue, Yarm came under Cleveland for administrative purposes. Yarm's name is said to come from an old word meaning fishpool – no doubt a dam was made to enable fish to be caught in one of the many loops of the Tees. It is recorded in the Domesday Book, and the position of the Church of St. Mary Magdalene on the river bank, a little away from the market place, and the grid system of streets and wynds all suggest that a small port existed before the creation of the borough which was already in existence in 1273. In 1295 burgesses were called upon to return a member to parliament. Before this date, the Blackfriars had a house and the hospital of St. Nicholas had been founded before 1148 by the second Robert de Brus, the Lord of the Manor of Yarm.

As you enter Yarm from the south, round a bend in the road, you see immediately one of the widest High Streets in Yorkshire, if not in England. The streets and wynds leave it at right angles on BOTH sides and all lead to the river! Elegant three storey mellow red brick houses appear straightaway on both sides, and were originally occupied by well-to-do merchants. Now, they are occupied very largely by professional firms of lawyers, and accountants and have very dignified entrances.

The wide open thoroughfare is a busy one, and on each side is a cobbled area large enough for at least three cars to be parked side by side between the road and the sidewalk. Smack in the middle of this busy and prosperous looking street is the old Town Hall with its clock and weather vane. It has stood four square in that position since 1710 and on its south side is the following legend:

1825   1925

To the Memory of
FIVE PIONEERS OF THE
FIRST PUBLIC RAILWAY
IN THE WORLD

Thomas Meynall (Chairman) of Yarm
Benjamin Flounders   "
Jeremiah Cairn   "
Richard Miles   "

Thomas M. Lee   "
Erected by the Inhabitants of Yarm.

Inset at the top is a small illustration of an old steam loco. The Rocket?

Immediately above the right-hand arch of the Town Hall is a plaque telling that there was an abnormal flood on 17th September 1771 – the height of the water is shown by a line which appears to be several feet above the average man's height. In this case, the river must have risen several feet before it entered the town streets. There is another high water mark some three to four feet above street level at a later date. A dam, which is said to have existed at one time, would not help to avoid flooding! It is easy to imagine that extreme flood waters would take a short cut across the many loops of the river especially that which almost encircles Yarm.

The broad High Street saw traffic from York on the old north road via Boroughbridge on its way to Durham. It is slightly curved and seems to be about one third of a mile long and is used to accommodate a Thursday market and annual fairs, where instead of the countless motor vehicles we see today, were cattle and horses. A market or fair was first held in the town as far back as 1207 in the reign of King John. It was held early in each year and continued until the late nineteenth century, but the October Fair is still held, at four different parts of the town. It is duly proclaimed on the second morning.

As we walk along the street, we cannot fail to notice more dignified and very attractive looking houses and shops as well as inns. At the top is No.124, a Georgian edifice with three ground floor bay windows and Venetian window. The next is an inn of special note – the Ketton Ox which is over 400 years old. It was a coaching inn and a central archway leads to the former stables. It has no connection with the Ketton in the Rutland/Northants area, but with Ketton near Darlington – this bull weighed 1 ton 14 cwt. and its meat would have provided the rations for 2,300 people in 1949 just before rationing was relaxed. The inn has six pilasters and an unusual feature is the row of oval windows on the top storey. They looked onto the cock-fighting pits made illegal in 1849. They are now bricked up and cemented over.

No.76 is intriguing and has three gabled dormers, possibly seventeenth century, and directly opposite is a charming Manor House, with bays on each side of one of the most attractive doorways in the street. On the east side again, there is the Union Arms, dated 1762. There are many others including two which are the same type as the Ketton Ox. We cannot leave the High Street without entering the George and Dragon, another ancient hostelry. A very important meeting was held here in the Commercial Room on 12th February 1820. Thomas Hill of Yarm presided at the meeting of the promoters of the Stockton and Darlington Railway, the first steam powered railway in the world. A plaque on the wall near the entrance reminds us of this momentous event. Indoors are framed old photographs showing ancient locos. Part of the modern plaster on the inside walls in the front

The Ketton Ox, Yarm

parlour has been carefully removed to reveal the original structure of wooden framework and brickwork for all to see. Old fashioned alcoves can be occupied for a quiet drink or snack.

At the south end of the High Street among the trees is The Friarage, a lovely building nearly 250 years old. It has a rather special porch with Tuscan columns, and surmounting the second floor is a balustrade with vases at the corners. It stands on the site of the Yarm house of the Blackfriars mentioned earlier.

Just off the High Street, near the Friarage, is a way down to the river called Atlas Wynd where a new development of housing has taken place. Still standing adjacent to this development is the old granary, brick built with smallish windows on three floors – thankfully preserved as a reminder of the old days. If you happen to be near the river bank, don't be surprised to see a large pleasure craft cruising up or down stream.

If we follow the footpath upstream soon we come to a tastefully built promenade. On the opposite side of the river are green fields and lovely trees, no longer hidden by the sails and masts of merchant ships. Since about 1840, Stockton and Middlesbrough have taken away Yarm's trade because modern ocean going ships could no longer make it as far upstream as Yarm. The first bridge over the Tees upstream from the coast was there – known as Shirlaw's Bridge (c.1400), so it is easy to see why Yarm became an important centre. In the Middle Ages, the town with its bridge and wharves, saw shipping to Scotland and France as well as to and from the Low Countries. Among exports were wool, hides and salt. Imports included terracotta tiles (pantiles) from Holland. Immediately south of the town is the road from Richmond along which came pigs of lead, and later, corn and firkins of butter for transport to the London area, by sea, of course. Yarm was a centre of linen weaving and cloth making, and even ship building took place.

The new promenade which replaced the once active wharves and shipping, leads up to the famous Shirlaw's Bridge, but let us first look to our left and explore the most unusual Methodist Chapel. It is octagonal and Wesley considered it to be 'by far the most elegant in England'. Here another wynd leads us back to the High Street, but continuing up the riverside path, one has a picturesque view of the famous old bridge of stone. From downstream, one sees the rounded arches of the period when the bridge was widened. Pass through the first arch by means of the footpath and there comes into view the bridge as it was originally, with pointed arches. If you stand back a little to have a full view, a beautiful background appears with the tower of Egglescliffe church showing above the trees.

Turn about, and confronting one is the enormous railway viaduct of stone crossing the river at a great height. Below the centre of the parapet is a large carved stone in the shape of a shield which bears the following legend:

Engineers
Thomas Grainger and John Bourne
Superintendent
Joseph Dixon
Contractors
Crowsdale Jackson and Garrow
1846

So, for the past 150 years, trains have gone to and fro high above the Tees. The old station serving Yarm near the south end of the viaduct of no less than 42 arches was closed some years ago, but a brand new one with a very large car park has been placed a little further south. Yarm is thus connected by rail, once again, to York, Leeds, Bradford and Halifax and on to Manchester and Liverpool, as well as to Middlesbrough and the north, and Whitby.

All roads made their way via Yarm because of the bridge and to the town because of its position. An important and fast road is from Yarm's counterpart as an inland port, Selby, the A19. Curiously enough, Selby is situated on the outside edge of its river, the Ouse, and Yarm is, or rather was, entirely within the loop of its river, Tees.

No wonder then that there were no less than 16 inns in Yarm 150 years ago. A lively place to stop and obtain refreshment. Alas, only six remain, but the town is becoming a place to visit and live in, and who knows, a revival could

Yarm Town Hall and High Street

be in sight. A little known coaching road led to Yarm from the Hambleton Hotel fairly near the top of Sutton Bank. Long disused, but a grand walk and well worth discovering.

Whilst some of the old houses and inns have become retail shops, it is only the ground floor that has been 'modernised' and one has only to raise the eyes a little to see the buildings as they were so long ago. However, the ancient wynds down to the river on both sides of the High Street are still intact for one to explore, though one is called Silver Street and not only leads to the modern riverside promenade, but to a modern supermarket car park!!

Almost opposite the Town Hall on the east side of High Street is Church Wynd. This leads to West Street and on the other side of the latter is the church of St. Mary Magdalene with its unique East Window looking across the gravestones to the street and the arches of the railway viaduct, now mostly of brick. The church is quite unusual, the east end being Georgian and the west being Norman, and a very curious Norman in at the bargain. The west tower appears to be the upper half of a very strange west front of Norman origin. The whole has been sandblasted and the stonework has a fresh look. Also the windows have been renewed; the most striking is the almond-shaped one near the top. There is a narrow one lower down and near the base is an almost square one. All three windows are built in a projection set against the main front which contains two small windows. Then there are north and south buttresses. Norman arches from windows are built into the north side of the north buttress. A more modern addition has been made to the south. Entry to this intriguing Norman part of the church is made through the modern addition or from the body of the church itself. What then does this west end of the church contain? The Sacristy, spiral staircases and bell cote are set among stone work some of which is over 800 years old. The almond shaped window which we have seen from the outside is thirteenth century and once opened to the nave. The tower, said to be fifteenth century, obviously blocked the view of the 'almond' window from the nave. Having viewed this unusual west front with great interest, one turns about and is surprised to find the river Tees just over the wall.

Inside the main building which is mainly early eighteenth century, we find a nave of five bays with two doorways on the south side, but there is much Victorian influence. However, standing on the chancel step, one is attracted immediately by the East Window, with its early Georgian surrounds which consist of fluted Corinthian pilasters. Rather unusual, but here again the stained glass has a Victorian look about it. Nevertheless it is very striking. There is on the south side a striking Georgian window with Moses standing under a canopy on a plinth of acanthus. Moses is in a robe of rich dark blue and red. Near this window is the font which consists of highly polished stone and concave sides. The font cover is very ornamental and could be Jacobean.

It is a pity that the effigies of a Knight and his Lady, most certainly fourteenth century, are placed on the floor near the main south door and in a position not easily seen by a visitor. A unique church.

As we leave the churchyard by means of the right hand path, we note the original site of Conyers School which was founded in Yarm as far back as 1590, without the arches of that gigantic viaduct overlooking it. Yet another landmark in that unique town's history.

RICHMOND

It matters not which approach is made to this famous Yorkshire town. One is always intrigued and looking forward to arriving, and surely never disappointed. In fact, having arrived in the largest horseshoe market place in England, there is such a variety of 'musts', that one often wonders which way to turn first.

Richmond does not appear to have warranted an entry in the Domesday Book, possibly because there was little of significance at that romantic spot when the Normans arrived. Nevertheless, William of Normandy granted Richmondshire area to Alan the Red, a relative of the Duke of Brittany, who in 1071 began to build the castle on that commanding position overlooking the river Swale. The castle does not appear to have had any battles or sieges to withstand, though as a stronghold it would have certainly held its own if circumstances had arisen. Perhaps the very strength of it would have discouraged any attempt, even by Cromwell himself. In any case, it had fallen into decay by the time he had made his name.

Henry VII (1546–1509) was Earl of Richmond from his birth, and after he became King in 1471 he built his palace on the Thames at Sheen (Shene), and renamed it Richmond. Here we might mention that one Frances (Fanny) I'Anson of Richmond, Yorkshire, married in 1787 Leonard McNally who composed the words 'Sweet Lass of Richmond Hill' for the music of that famous song. The house where she lived, Hill House, stands high up above the main road to Darlington, just past the top of Frenchgate and the junction of Anchorage Hill and Maison Dieu. There is a raised sidewalk, and steps to a stone archway leading to the house, aptly named. A portrait of Frances hangs in the ballroom at the top of the stairs in the Kings Head Hotel in the market place.

The town was not missed by Henry VIII's antiquary, John Leland, who in the sixteenth century wrote:

> "There is a Chapel in Richmond Towne with straung Figures in the Walles of it. The peple there dreme that it was (a temple of) Idoles.
> Richmond Towne is waullid. Waullid it was but the Waul is now decayed. The Names and Parts of 4 or 5 Yates yet remain Frenchegate yn the North Parte of the Towne and is the most occupied Gate of the Towne. Finkel-streete Gate, Bargate. All iii be downe."

Like Pontefract, Richmond with its castle also perched high up on top of an enormous outcrop of rock, is a town with a strong continental flavour. Richmond, however, is surrounded by some unrivalled scenery, and at its feet is the very romantic river Swale, the longest of all Yorkshire Dales rivers.

Here we are then, standing in that curiously shaped market place with Holy Trinity Church set almost on the middle. Curiously enough, the first thing we notice on the church stonework is a nameplate bearing the legend HOLY

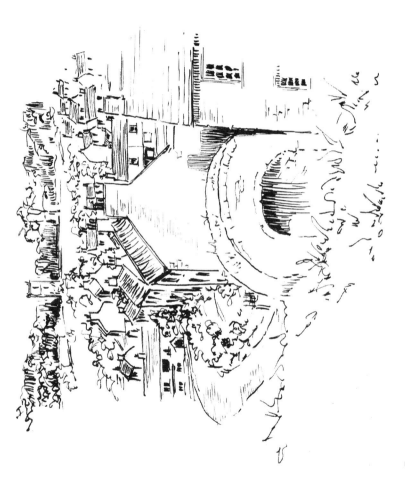

Bargate & Culloden Tower, Richmond

TRINITY SQUARE! At one period in the church's history there were several shops occupying the north aisle. Continental flavour again. Today, The Green Howards military museum has taken over the shops and much of the church itself. It is well worth a visit. Shops still adjoin the east end of the church but are not part of it.

The age old tower with a list to starboard holds the clock which goes on reminding us that time waits for no man, or woman for that matter! Services are held in part of the church's south side – the times and days are given on a prominent notice on the south wall for all to see.

Let us see what is left of Leland's "4 or 5 Yates". Leading from the market place is Friars Wynd – a narrow little street which soon becomes a mere archway, through which and indeed above which we can see Greyfriars Tower. This archway is one of the two remaining 'Yates' and on the side of the wall at the side we learn the following:

FRIARS WYND

Set in one of the remaining sections
of the town wall. Built circa 1313

This gateway and wynd gave access to
the Franciscan Friary church from
the Market Place.

Resurfaced by Richmondshire District
Council 1978

Passing through this archway, just wide enough for a couple walking close together, but with plenty of headroom, the full length of the Friary Tower appears before us. It stands in a cared for garden with well, and from a distance gives the impression of perfection as it must have done centuries ago. Sadly, on close inspection the ravages of time and weather and perhaps a little neglect, are quite apparent. However, close inspection reveals substantial remains of the church, but none of the offices' remains appear on the large area of grassland ahead of one.

Nearby is the modern information centre – open every day except Saturday afternoon and Sunday.

Opposite is the Georgian Theatre built in 1788. It has had an up and down career – it was even used as a furniture storeroom and also an auction room. However, for some years now, it has served its original purpose and is a venue for theatre-goers from far and near. Considering its rough passage, it has survived as possibly the best example of such a theatre in the whole of England. The proscenium is almost perfect. Ground floor boxes are still there as well as the upper boxes supported on Tuscan columns. The pay box, stage, dressing rooms and staircase are original. If Shakespeare were alive today, he would surely approve of it wholeheartedly. Well known artistes play their parts there regularly.

If we turn left into Victoria Road and explore the area beyond, as well as Newbiggin, we find many houses of distinction of the Georgian and Victorian periods. One can easily picture a colourful scene with horse-drawn carriages bearing theatre-goers from that area for an evening's entertainment and perhaps a supper afterwards at the Kings Head. It is still done of course, but without the horses! The Kings Head is one of the very few former houses in the market place not to have had its ground floor frontage changed to modern style shop-fronts. It is of the early eighteenth century period with eight bays and one original doorway. We can only hope that it stays that way.

Back in the market place, let us now have a look at the other remaining gate of the old town wall. To the west is New Road, down which we venture, but for only a short distance because we turn left down a narrow lane and just as we do so, a most attractive view appears. In the foreground is the steep hill with its houses perched almost on top of each other, but beyond is a green area of rising ground. Smack in the middle is a remarkable tower, (Culloden Tower, in fact) erected some 250 years ago to commemorate the defeat of the Jacobites. It consists of a very high and well-built octagon resting on a square base. Attractively built of stone with pointed windows, it has three main floors. The room on the first floor has a remarkable chimney piece. The second floor is quite different and is somewhat classical. This is typical of Richmond as so often one is distracted from one's original objective by some other eye-catching place, whether it is a lovely house, cottage, abbey ruins or just a view of views . . . So let us go down the little cobbled lane, and just before reaching the gate we see a plaque on the wall which tells us:

> THIS NARROW LANE called THE BAR or BARR after
> the adjoining postern gate in the Town Walls
> Built c.1312 on account of Scottish incursions
> The postern gave access from the old bridge to
> the Market Place for pedestrians and packhorses

It is larger than the postern at Friars Wynd and consists of a simple high arch, stonework showing on the town side and part cement rendering on the outward side. The lane, Cornforth Hill, is still very steep and the houses on the right hand side have a wee bit of a French look about them. Lower down, we join Bridge Street and the Green, Bargate Green, in fact. A pleasant place which seems far away from the hurly burly of the Market Place, and apart from the traffic coming and going from the river bridge, is a quiet spot. So different from the past, when there was a corn mill, a fulling mill, a dyeworks, a tannery and even a brewery. Full use was naturally made of the river. The bridge nearby, known as the Green Bridge, has three graceful arches with semi-circular cut waters. It has the stamp of John Carr who was responsible for so many elegant structures in York and the old North Riding especially. Rebuilding took place early in the nineteenth century when the bridge was widened. Leland, in his itinerary, said it had four arches in the sixteenth century and Speed, that great cartographer, agreed with this in 1610, but in October 1739, the Sessions discussed a contract for repairs. 'Discussed' seems as far as it got, until many years later.

To obtain the famous postcard view of the bridge and castle, one has to cross the river and proceed upstream a hundred yards or so along a well trodden path and then turn round. No wonder countless artists and photographers come this way. Afternoon is a good time. If we carry on a little further upstream, Round Howe appears, an isolated hill with trees on top which seems to have been cut off from the adjacent hill or cliff side during the glacial period, leaving a semi-circular space between it and the hillside. On the way back to the bridge you will notice a rift in the rock which is known as Arthur's Oven. There is no record of any cakes having been burnt there, either by Arthur or even King Alfred himself.

To obtain another view of Richmond, but perhaps without the bridge, one should climb up the steep road to Scotton. After a breathless few hundred yards, turn round and behold a spectacular view of views. Returning downhill to the bridge, notice on the downstream parapet, a slab which tells every traveller that it is 18 miles to ASKRIGG, and that LANCASTER is 56 miles away, along the old turnpike road which was opened in 1751.

Back in town, we must surely climb the castle keep as well as have a walk round the inner bailey. To reach it, we make for the Town Hall which is opposite the south side of the church. It has an unusually large porch and the eastern half of the building is the Town Hall Hotel and along its eastern end is the road which leads to the castle. There are some mighty castle keeps in Yorkshire, but Conisbrough and Richmond can claim that theirs are just about intact and are both about the same height (approx. 100 feet). They have stood for 800 years despite wind, rain and storm as well as some neglect in the past, and both look good for another 800 years. A strenuous climb within the 11 feet thick walls leads us to the parapets from which the whole of Richmond and its surroundings stand below our very feet. The points of interest abound and one can spend much time identifying them all. On the way down, we now take notice of the chambers on each floor. On the first floor is a pillar in the middle supporting the floor above – absent on the next floor. The well which supplied water for those living in the keep was through an archway on the ground floor, but to keep the supply safe, access to the well was later blocked up and the stonework was carried up to the first floor from which buckets were lowered.

The original and smaller keep was in the south corner of the great court, now a huge lawn-like inner bailey. It is called Scolland's Hall which served both as a residence and defence point. It was not until about a hundred years later that the present huge keep was built. As we approach Scolland's Hall we pass on our left the remains of St. Nicholas Chapel, one of three in the castle, then from the corner of the inner bailey, a glorious view of the river and old bridge comes into view. Herringbone masonry and other styles suggest that the curtain wall and the original gatehouse as well as Scolland's Hall were completed towards the end of the eleventh century. The Hall is the earliest example of this type of domestic occupation within a castle courtyard in the whole of Europe. It will be seen that it stands two storeys high and the main rooms on the first floor were reached by an outdoor staircase.

At the foot of the outer walls there is a broad pathway, a most attractive one, approached from Castle Terrace off Millgate. Below is the Swale winding its way round the high cliffs, sometimes just murmuring, at other times dashing madly over its rocky bed. Trees flourish. Whilst ruminating on one of the many seats along the path, one thinks of that young man, Peter Thompson, who came across a way to the entrance of a fabulous chamber under the castle's foundations in which King Arthur and his Knights slept with the sword Excalibur and a jewelled horn beside them. Peter picked up these, but quickly dropped them when he saw Arthur and his Knights appeared to be rising out of their slumbers, he thereupon fled. He was in such a frightened state that he could not remember how he got there . . . and so, King Arthur and his entourage sleep on, just as they do in a cave just north of Hadrian's Wall at Sewing Shields. There, a farmer found a chamber in which King Arthur (and his Queen, this time) lay in a state of complete enchantment.

As soon as the farmer cut loose the King's garter, the whole company began to awaken. He had only to blow the horn to waken them completely, but here again he became scared to death and left the horn unblown, leaving the cave in a great hurry without remembering where he made his discovery – like Peter Thompson. Whilst Richmond and Sewing Shields are a far cry from Tintagel, Winchester, Avalon or Glastonbury, it is reliably reported that King Arthur was born at Mallerstang, on the Yorkshire/Westmorland border, so perhaps this part of Northern England may claim with some justification to be associated with this fascinating legend.

Let us stand for a few minutes at the highest point in the market place. Here we have an obelisk with stupa-like surfaces (slightly convex) which rests on a base with pedimented niches and surmounted by a large stone ball. It was erected in 1771 in place of the priceless original market cross which consisted of a high flight of steps which led in turn to a square platform enclosed by a richly ornamented wall some six feet high, having buttresses at the corners, each surmounted by a dog sitting on its hind legs. Within the wall rose the cross with a shaft of stone. There were many curious compartments in the wall and an archway which led out into the square. It is said that shields bearing the arms of four well known families were carved on the stonework. Alas, the march in the name of progress! Obviously the original cross must have taken up much more room than its successor. The same fate overtook the original '4 or 5 yates' of Leland's day, but as we have already seen Bargate and Friars Wynd have survived. It must be admitted that if the archways of the original town walls were anything like those at Bargate or Friars Wynd, access to and from a growing town would be seriously hampered, especially for wheeled traffic at say, the end of Frenchgate and its adjoining wall. One can easily imagine men of influence in Richmond saying, 'Let us remove these obstacles to trade and progress. If we are to keep Richmond as an important trading centre for lead, wool, skins, hay, straw, knitted goods, butter, cattle, sheep and corn, for example, we need easy access'. The bars at York were a very different matter as wheeled traffic had little difficulty in those days in passing through them. However, this cannot surely be the reason for the demolishing of the old market cross.

We cannot leave the subject of trade in Richmond without reference to the numerous guilds. Throughout the Middle Ages no less than 13 trade guilds controlled the business life of the town until at least 1821. Fifteen years after that all had disappeared except the mercers, haberdashers and grocers. The Company of Fellmongers was revived in 1982 and included skinners and glovers; some of the old ceremonies have been revived including a ceremonial dinner which takes place each year.

Our last sally from the market place must be to Frenchgate in which the non-military French lived after the building of the castle. It is a steep street with many attractive houses of the Georgian period. Several have lovely porches with Tuscan columns and pediments. Swale House was the home of James Tate, the Master of the Grammar School. At this house, Lewis Carroll, the author of *Alice in Wonderland* and many other writings, stayed when he was a student at the school. Near the top of Frenchgate is a public house with a delightful English name – The Ship! At the very top is a flight of steps leading to a memorial to the men of the Green Howards who lost their lives in World War I and again in World War II. A few more steps take us into Pottergate, across which to our left is the imposing Oglethorpe House at the corner of Gallowgate. Nearby is Hill House where Frances I'Anson the sweet lass is said to have lived. Gallowgate leads to the former race course on a plateau about a mile from the town centre. It dates back to 1775. Imposing gate – set in a lay by suggest its one-time fame.

It is worthwhile walking from Pottergate into the Darlington Road to have a look at the 'Bowes Hospital'. It was an almshouse founded way back in 1607 with a chapel of St Edmund. Much of the original stonework is visible from the road and bits of Norman carving have been re-set.

A little further on the Darlington Road, we see a complete change from the ancient to modern in the shape of Richmond High School for Girls. A functional yet very comfortable building, it is intricate and unexpected. Although dating back to just before World War II, it has the stamp of modern architecture of 40 years later.

Let us return to Frenchgate. Half-way down on the left is Church Wynd. This very steep wynd leads directly to the Parish Church of St Mary. Incidentally, it is situated outside the old town walls and most of the building dates from 1399. Just outside the North Porch is the Grave Cover of a fourteenth century eccle-siastic, the chalice denoting his office. Inside there are many features of interest including the Green Howards Chapel at the entrance to which is an ancient font, Norman, rescued from the churchyard where it lay sunk catching water from a spring. The Green Howards regiment was established in November 1688 and so covers a period of 300 years of campaigns and wars and, of course, has links with the men and women of Richmond and Teesside. In the sanctuary is a thirteenth century oak aumbry, used to hold sacred vessels. It is particularly rare and apart from its hoary appearance it has double doors.

The star attractions in the interior of the church, in the opinion of many, are the back rows of the Choir Stalls. These were rescued from Easby Abbey, a mile out of town, at the Dissolution of 1535. On the canopy is a Latin inscription which translated in English, reads

THERE ARE TEN KINDS OF MISCHIEF IN THE CLOISTER.

Extravagant living; exquisite food,
gossip in church, quarrelling amongst
the clergy; disorderliness in the
choir; idle students, disobedience in
the young; complacency in the old;
obstinacy amongst the religious and
worldliness amongst ministers.

The Easby stalls have Misericordes, seats which lift to provide a ledge for older ministers to lean against as they stand through lengthy litanies. Some of the carvings on these mercy seats are far from pious. For example, there is a carving of a pig playing bagpipes!

Back into Frenchgate we find our way into Ryders Wynd and the Richmondshire Museum which is run on a voluntary basis, and open from Easter to October inclusive. Apart from displays of local history there are many photographs of the town before the advent of the motor car, as well as relics of the leadmining and farming activities. One should not fail to miss the Vets' surgery from the B.B.C. series *All creatures great and small* featuring James Herriot. A dog squatting on the operating table completes the picture.

As we leave the town centre we notice a street with the curious name, Maison Dieu, the French influence is here to stay! There are two ways to visit Easby Abbey and Church. By road, we pass the site of St. Nicholas Hospital, a hospice used by pilgrims and other travellers to and from the Abbey. Today, a seventeenth century house stands in several acres of grounds. Apart from an extensive and very trim series of yew tree hedges, rhododendrons and the like grow in wild profusion and in the late spring are extremely colourful. Lovely views from well placed pathways appear from time to time to give the visitor some idea of the wonderful position of the place overlooking the river far below. These grounds are open to the public and there is an honesty box on the premises!

Soon we turn to the right and find ourselves at Easby Abbey. The first thing

we pass by is the Gatehouse, almost intact. The Abbey was founded by one
Roald, a constable of Richmond Castle about 1150 and the white robed monks
were of the Premonstratensian order and a great deal of their time was spent
in farming. Abbeys of this Order were founded at Coverham in Yorkshire and
outside Yorkshire we find an Abbey at Egglestone and at Blanchland in Durham
to mention two not too distant. Much of the south side of the Abbey stands well,
the beautiful east window, too. One is sometimes puzzled with the irregularity
of the positioning of some of the buildings – this is due to the fact that the
reredorter and dormitory were built on the skew on account of the proximity of
the river. Also it will be seen that the cloister is far from being the more usual
square. It is considered that the best overall view of the Abbey is from across
the river. Evidently, the famous artist, J.M.W. Turner thought so way back in
1816. There is a lovely painting by him of the abbey in the British Museum
based on a pencil drawing done at that time.

Between the Gatehouse and the Abbey, stands Easby church. It is thought that
it was established before the advent of the Abbey. Apart from the chancel little
of the original church remains. However, we can go back to the thirteenth century
with some certainty. Entry to this attractive long low church can be gained at
reasonable hours during the day by way of the lovely old porch. A feature indoors
is the painting of subjects from the New and Old Testaments on the south and
north walls respectively. Apart from the clergy, very few people could read or
write 700 years ago and so the gospel was taught visually! Considering that these
wall paintings were done in the thirteenth century, they have stood the test of
time remarkably well. We learn that the water colours were laid on the plaster
before the latter was dry, so that the paint would be more than skin deep.

Another rather unique attraction of Easby Church is its famous cross. Near the
north chancel wall is a plaster cast of the Northumbrian cross, it appears that the
original was considered rather crude and was broken up and some of it used in
repairing the walls of the church itself. Another part was kept in the grounds of
Easby Hall for many years. Eventually all the parts were put together forming a
complete cross. The front shows Christ with his disciples and the back consists
of carvings of animals and birds. The whole is now in the Victoria and Albert
Museum. It seems a pity that the original which dates back to early eighth century
should not remain in Easby, but the money received from its sale was put to
good use in the church itself. There are many features apart from the cross which
attract attention, such as the sedilia. As we leave, we cannot fail to notice the
elaborate Norman font near which is an entrance to a room over the porch reached
by a stone staircase.

As we make our way back to Richmond along the footpath near the river, we
feel rather sad that so many of those ancient stones, quarried, shaped and carved
by those dedicated men should finish up, after years of work on them, as a pile
of rubble following the Dissolution. But even if subsequent looting and plundering
of the stonework left the place more desolate than ever, surely some of those

precious stones would have been put to some use to help to build some place of beauty and or romance. Who knows? There must be surely someone who proudly possesses a stone or stones which came from Easby.

When we reach the modern swimming pool and former attractively built railway station, the road to Catterick Garrison leads us uphill. After a few hundred yards, on the left hand side is a building seemingly consisting of ancient stones which attracts our attention. We venture through a gateway into a paved yard and find a delightful little tower with a doorway with continuous chamfers. There are two perpendicular windows. This is what remains of St. Martin's Priory, a small Benedictine House. It stands there in the sunshine and the rain apparently oblivious of time. One wonders how few visitors it has because there is no sign near the entrance, but wait! Across the road is a newish private road and some pleasant houses on its sides. Inevitably, it has the word 'priory' as part of its description. The views of Richmond from here are quite superb, and with that lovely panoramic vista in our minds, we take our leave of that quite unique town.

DENT

Is there a town besides Dent which can boast of wall to wall cobbles forming its winding main streets?

There are several ways of approaching the town. The Settle-Carlisle Railway, famous for the scenic route it takes to reach Carlisle, crosses the head of Dentdale, and if the appropriate train is taken, it will stop at Dent Station. On alighting one obtains a quite unique view of the dale as it bends to the south-west and then turns a little towards the north-west. To one's horror, one is told that it is about four and a half miles to the town. This sounds a bit much because there is no public transport, but in fact the time taken to do the walk is all too short as there are so many attractions on the way.

The second approach, by road this time, is from the main Ingleton to Hawes road at Newby Head. On leaving the main road, you descend alongside a gill and pass under a railway arch and shortly have Dent Head viaduct immediately on your right. It is well worth stopping here to have a close look at the enormous size and indeed workmanship of the marble blocks which form the bases of the piers of those lofty railway arches. Most of them stand on a natural base of Dent marble. On passing under the arches, one is pleasantly surprised to see, just ahead, the almost complete remains of an ancient pack-horse bridge spanning the beck before it passes under the viaduct and road bridge to join the infant river Dee. It is grass grown and without parapets, but it is still a very convenient way of crossing the beck on foot.

Here and hereabouts, Dent marble was quarried for many years. There were two kinds – black, or nearly so, and marled grey which when cut and polished in a building near Stone House Bridge, lower down the valley, found its way as far as the Inns of Court in London, the Cartwright Hall in Bradford as well as a very beautiful staircase at Owens College in Manchester. Nearer home, one finds the chancel in Dent church paved with grey and black marble. Alas 1808 saw the last of marble cut and polished in the Stone House works, owing to the relaxation of import duty on marble especially from Italy. Sometimes, Dent marble is put in inverted commas because it consists of fossilized crinoids combined with Hardraw Scar limestone!

As we go down the steep road, the infant Dee is at our side, slipping along limestone ledges and falling down from one to another. When we approach Stone House Bridge it is good to pause awhile and go up the lane to the right where in addition to Stone House Farm, there are several attractive houses with natural gardens which follow the contours. This is the foot of Arten Gill and ahead is Arten Gill viaduct silhouetted against the pale northern sky – eleven arches.

To continue down the valley of the Dee, we have to cross one of the narrowest of road bridges ever. One is warned of this some two and a half miles back on Newby Head.

The Adam Sedgwick Drinking Fountain, Dent

Having successfully negotiated Stone House Bridge, we come to the first inn in the dale and then to the hamlet of Lea Yeat with its delightful one-arched bridge, to the right is the infamous steep and winding road up to the railway station. There is an old story about a stranger, who, on having dashed up the valley from Dent town to catch a train, beheld 'Station Road'; he asked a local chap why the Midland Railway had built the station such a long way away. The reply: "They thought it best to have the station alongside the railway lines." Not a bad idea!

Lea Yeat was visited by the famous quaker, George Fox, who was responsible for the building of a Friends Meeting House in the late seventeenth century. Such was George Fox's enthusiasm that over three hundred years ago he found his way to tiny Lea Yeat, in those days a very remote area indeed. The building is still to be seen, but it is no longer a Quaker meeting house.

Down the valley then to Cowgill. It is the tiniest of hamlets with yet another bridge, on the parapet of which is a stone slab proclaiming:

THIS BRIG REPERED AT THE CHARGE
OF THE WEST RIDING A.D. 1702

Just here is an equally ancient little lane which takes one over the hill to Garsdale. There also is a modern church dedicated to St. John; it was constructed on the site of a former Presbyterian chapel, and later used by the sect known as The Sandemanians founded by a Scotsman, John Glass, who it is said was suspended for heresy. He felt that the church and state should not be connected in any way and that justification of the faith meant nothing more than a simple assent to the divine mission of Christ. Many customs of the Sandemanians included the Kiss of Charity, the use of the lot and weekly love-feasts. John Glass and George Fox must have created quite a stir in Cowgill and neighbouring Lea Yeat in those far off days!

After crossing the 'repered' bridge over the stream, there is yet another to our left which crosses the Dee and is called Ewegales Bridge; here we have a choice of delightful routes to Dent town. Not far downstream, the river has cut through the limestone and formed a deep gorge-like channel, and by peering over the barrier from the right-hand road just past a cottage named 'Stone Croft', we see two waterfalls, the lower one of which is called Hud's Foss. To reach it, it is better to speak to the farmer at Ewegales on the opposite side of the river. Just below the Foss, are the remains of a hosiery mill, and later a brewery, used to supply the needs of the men engaged in the construction of the railway. The Foss is not a grand one, but is very attractive, as is the setting.

Lower downstream is a footbridge, Nelly Brig, easily approached from a lay-by and which leads across the deeply fissured limestone bed of the river. The latter is usually dry as the water has found its way under the present bed. Across the river is a path which leads straight up to the road on the south side. Immediately downstream is a water worn gorge down which the water dashes over and into

Denthead Viaduct

a chasm containing a very deep pool; it is known as Ibby Peril. Wild flowers abound, especially primroses in the spring.

Lower down still is Hell Cauldron, best approached from the road on the south side from a spot called Tub Hole from which a path goes down to a stream crossed by means of a substantial plank, round the top of a huge rocky depression, and down to the river where a well made footbridge gives access to the north bank. This bridge overlooks a fantastically fissured river bed both upstream and down. A bronze plate on the north side of the bridge tells us that:

THIS BRIDGE WAS ERECTED BY

No.140 Airmen Aircrew
initial training course
from Royal Air Force
Finningley
on 27–28 June 1987

Here we make use of the bridge and gain a well defined footpath downstream by the riverside. Very soon the fissured limestone disappears and the waters come to the surface, to accompany us as far as Tommy Bridge, yet another wooden affair for pedestrians only. Once across this to the sorth side of the river, there is a choice of paths to Dent town. Here also the valley has widened out and the waters of Deepdale join the Dee.

Once in Dent town, we find ourselves in one of the quaintest places outside Cornwall. Thick soled shoes or boots make walking easier over the cobbles. It is easy to imagine the tumbrel cart of old rumbling its way through the town, as the poet Coleridge described some 150 years ago:

> Narrow and winding are its rattling streets
> Where cart with cart in cumbrous conflict meets.

The tumbrel was used particularly in Dentdale, and was 'home made'. The two wheels revolved with the axle and not on it, and consisted of solid wood, prevented from slipping off the axle by means of a simple peg. Shafts enabled the cart to be hauled by man or beast.

Before seeking refreshment at either the Sun Inn or the George and Dragon, or at one of the cosy cafés, we must visit the grand old church dedicated to St. Andrew. It has a Norman doorway in the north wall, now blocked. It was opposite the present entrance and gave access across the yard to the former grammar school, now flats for old people. The original Norman church stood as far as the present chancel steps. The sturdy tower was rebuilt some 200 years ago with the very same stones of the original Norman one which tumbled down some 15 years previously.

The beautifully carved seventeenth century box pews were removed when the church was thoroughly restored over 100 years ago, but a number, fortunately, have been retained and are placed against the former north wall doorway as well as at the end of north aisle and the south aisle. They were the family pews of the 24 sidesmen, a body of landowners way back to 1429. They still exist today, sharing with the Bishop of Bradford in the appointment of the vicar, and meeting annually to distribute ancient charities. At the end of the south aisle, too, is the actual desk and chair used by the Master of the Grammar School which was founded in the reign of James I.

The east window depicts the Te Deum and includes Christ and two Old Testament figures as well as 10 Christian saints. In the chancel at our feet are black and grey marble tiles from the Dentdale quarries. The south aisle window is a memorial to Revd. John Sedgwick appointed vicar in 1822 and remaining for 37 years, whilst a tablet in the church records that his son, Adam, was baptised there, but buried in the Chapel of Trinity College, Cambridge. After attending the little grammar school in Dent, later at Sedbergh school, he entered Cambridge in 1803. He was appointed Woodwardian professorship of geology, a post he held almost to the end of his life in 1873.

There are seats in the northern part of the churchyard which give superb views, both across the valley and up and down stream. Sit there awhile and wonder why serenity such as one experiences here cannot spread throughout the world. After leaving this delectable spot and entering busy main roads again one knows full well why it does not.

The two inns, the Sun and the George and Dragon are less than a stone's throw apart, and halfway between the two or nearly so is a huge block of hewn Shap granite and a basin of the same material, which serve as a drinking fountain. It is inscribed with none other than Adam Sedgwick's name and relevant dates as seen in the church. Teetotallers are therefore provided for! But let it be known that Dent has its own brewery only a stone's throw from the George and Dragon. The Adam Sedgwick drinking fountain is a magnet for artists and photographers, especially as the cobbled street shows up well and part of the Sun Inn with its Sun face forms the background.

We used to hear about the 'Terrible Knitters of Dent'. What has happened to them? Knitting still takes place in Dent, but not as it did in those far off days. Dent folk, male and female, would gather in groups at a chosen house, in rotation. Tales were told, songs were sung against the click-click of the needles. Stockings, caps, night caps and even jackets were produced and some were sold as far away as Kendal market. There was no doubt about it, Dent had a great name in the world of knitting.

For many years, Dent has been the Mecca for the walker and the naturalist. It still is and even though there is now a Pay and Display car and picnic spot to the west of this unique and little town, the visitors, or most of them, depart and in the evening quietness descends almost as it has always done. Nevertheless, the now well known Dalesway from Ilkley to the English Lake District makes its way into Dentdale and its many natural attractions. There is forestry at the head of the valley and south of Lea Yeat, and a profusion of rare and common wild flowers, especially along the river banks, to give pleasure to those who are not in a hurry. For the more energetic there are many hills to climb. Whernside, the highest of the famous Three Peaks, can be approached from several points. For those less energetic, it is possible to motor up Deepdale to its highest point just over 1500 feet above sea level leaving only some 900 feet to climb on foot to reach the summit. Great Coum and Gragareth are easily reached by returning to the road and crossing over to reach the summits and look down that intriguing valley of Ease Gill.

Short walks abound in all directions from Dent town. One of these starts at the green just past the Old Vicarage and at the foot of Flintergill you turn right along a footpath to Dent's little sister, Gawthrop. Three quarters of a mile brings you to this charming place which tucks itself into the hillside's nooks and crannies. The first house of note is Gawthrop Hall perched on natural platform, the base of which is often gay with flowers. We soon meet the 'highway' from Dent and find it winds its way through the village and after crossing lovely little Haycote Bridge splits up – one way leads over the hill to Barbondale, the other carries on to Sedbergh. There are no side by side houses or cottages along the 'main street' because the dwellings have been built in a charmingly haphazard way. It gives the impression that building has taken place from time to time in cosy spots or on raised ground with a view, or else beside one of the two main becks which run down to the Dee. Many dwellings are whitewashed and have attractive gardens, both large and small. In spite of the apparent haphazard placing of the houses, there is always a way through from one to another, even if only a footpath. Of course, there is a telephone booth and post box, but no inn.

The views from Gawthrop are naturally of the dale, and in the background is Rise Hill to the north and east which is often bathed in sunshine. On top of the hill and Dinsdale Pike, one is fascinated with the stones comprising the walls, because, so often, they contain fossils of small animal or crustacean life. One is often tempted to pocket a small piece as a memento!

If we make our way down to the Dent-Sedbergh road, we cross Nettle Pot Gill – how did it get that name? – and reach an attractive crossing of the Dee by way of Barth Bridge with riverside footpaths. The other bridge is Rash Bridge, a well proportioned stone structure in wooded surroundings. Small corbels appear to give partial support to the parapets. There is much bird life, and fish abound at times in one particularly deep pool. A scramble down the river bank is quite rewarding. Rash Bridge can be reached direct from Gawthrop by means of a wee lane on the south side of the Dee. Instead of crossing the bridge to reach the main road to Sedbergh you may carry on taking the wee lane, grass grown in the middle, but tarmac on each side, to observe nature virtually undisturbed by man. Eventually the lane rises into open ground and becomes gated; then it crosses a substantial bridge over the former railway from Ingleton to Low Gill. Soon an 'Open Farm' is reached. Visitors are welcome to see the animals fed, cows milked, and in season, sheep sheared, and so on. As one approaches, one may well see perched on a low wall, a peacock showing off his lovely plumage.

The track carries on past the farm and eventually leads to the Kirkby Lonsdale/Sedbergh road. Turn right here and about halfway to Sedbergh you will sometimes notice a few parked cars on a small lay-by on the left. The reason? Just here a sign-post points down a narrow but inviting lane to Brigflatts, a hamlet near the river Rawthey and also a Friends Meeting House. Ancient cottages and houses stand among lovely old trees, and in a simple but attractive garden stands what must surely be one of the most comely Quaker Meeting Houses in the north of England. Its attraction is enhanced by the stone fronted porch – the sides are whitewashed as is the rest of the building. Inside, it is not as austere as one might think, and there is a gallery. To sit on one of the seats in that little garden and meditate whilst a meeting is taking place in the House, makes you consider the futility of war, but you are brought down to earth as well. There must surely be "punishment of wickedness and vice".

The date over the doorway is 1675. It seems incredible at first, that over 300 years ago, the indomitable George Fox preached in this very remote spot. It is said that he made Manchester a centre for a time then moved north to Kendal and made full use of the vast area round that town to put across his beliefs.

SEDBERGH

The north-west outpost of the Diocese of Bradford, Yorkshire and indeed the north-westerly outpost of the former West Riding of Yorkshire.

Granted market rights way back as far as 1150, the town is situated near the confluence of four valleys and rivers: Dentdale, Garsdale, the Rawthey valley and the Lune. Its importance lies in the fact that it was an almost essential stopping place between Kendal and Kirkby Stephen, and also the way to Wensleydale via Garsdale, whilst traffic to and from Dentdale naturally called at or passed through Sedbergh. In spite of its current importance, it has not outgrown itself over the years and the narrow main street retains, at least, some of its ancient charm together with its little Market Place by the north entrance to the Parish Church of St Andrew. This, of course is notwithstanding the 'disappearance' of the Market Cross over 100 years ago. The blacksmiths have long since gone and one smithy was replaced by the post office many years ago. Incidentally the Post Office has occupied a number of sites, and is at present on the north side of the main street, a little to the west of the Market Place, where a small market is held each Wednesday.

Sedbergh is a place to explore; visitors are often intrigued by the very names of the side streets, such as Joss Lane and Castlehaw Lane and, of course, there is the inevitable Finkle Street, the first section of the main road to Dent. If we go down Finkle Street a short distance, we come to an unusual attractively constructed building which arouses our curiosity. It is entered from Back Lane which is parallel with the main street. It consists of three floors and turns out to be none other than the Sedbergh School Library and is certainly well endowed with books. It stands on the site of the original school of 1525, rebuilt in 1716. Just below the building was a patch of land which was the school playground, ill-used or little used, it is said. It is now a welcome car park.

Some of the stones of the original school building were reused in the erection of the present library, and on the south side overlooking the car park, one of the stones was used by Adam Sedgwick to carve his name to which he added the date 1803. The carving is as clear today as it was nearly 200 years ago. It will be remembered that Adam was the son of the then vicar of Dent, and became a Woodwardian professor of geology at Cambridge. As a budding geologist he certainly chose the right kind of stone on which to carve his name. No rain or storm has worn it away in the slightest degree!

One Roger Lupton, a local boy born 1456, and awarded in 1483, a Bachelor of Law degree, King's College, Cambridge, served in the Chancery Court, was Canon of Windsor in 1500, became Provost of Eton College in 1503. To him we owe the beginnings of Sedbergh School in 1525, and by the end of two years six scholarships to St. John's Cambridge had been established. The school survived Henry VIII's plan to dissolve Chantry schools. This was due to the pleadings

Friends Meeting House at Brigflatts near Sedbergh

Sedbergh School

of St. John's College and a sermon from Dr. Lever, its Master, before the King, claiming that the school "was most needed in the north country amongst the rude people in knowledge". It became a Grammar School in 1551.

From then onwards there were successes and, sad to relate, some failures, but by the mid-eighteenth century, the successes of Sedbergh boys in Classics and Mathematics made the school famous at Cambridge. From 1876 the school really 'got going'. Sir Francis Sharp Powell, a Bradford man and an old boy (O.S.) was noted particularly for his generosity in providing funds for accommodation for the Head Master and Assistant Masters, as well as for boarders. Today, we have attractive Houses, Lupton House, Powell House, Winder House for example, and the superb building which accommodates, inter alia, the Headmaster's Study and School Offices. The parterre of this beautiful building is set immediately above a dignified arched arcade of cream stone in the cloister of which are panels bearing the names of Old Sedberghians who fell in the Great War and World War II. One cannot fail to note the outstandingly large number of young men whose names appear on those panels and stop for a moment's meditation.

The facilities for learning in all its forms as well as relaxation are manifold. In 1991 a new Coat of Arms to the school was granted and Queen Elizabeth and Prince Phillip paid a visit during which the new Sports Hall was opened. At the time of writing there are 340 boys at the school, only a handful are day boys. It has not admitted any girls, even to the top forms. Although boys of all religions, cultural and racial backgrounds are welcome, the whole school attends a Church of England service every Sunday in its own chapel. The latter was built about 100 years ago, and whilst the exterior is of a creamy grey coloured stone, the interior is of a warmer tone with a tinge of red. As soon as one enters one is struck with the beauty and size. It has a low arcaded nave with clerestory above, transepts and an impressive chancel with reredos. Many of the windows are glazed with scenes from the Annunciation, The Nativity, The Visitation and The Crucifixion. There are many plaques which include the names of the very many distinguished men, scholarships which have emanated from this once remote seat of learning.

You have to turn south along the Dent road and entrance to Sedbergh Golf Course, to discover Millthrop Bridge which crosses the river Rawthey. It is possible to overlook this grand bridge in a journey from Kendal or Kirkby Lonsdale to Kirkby Stephen because the main road passes through the main streets of Sedbergh. It is only when travelling to and fro between the town and Dentdale that this old river crossing has to be negotiated. It is in a beautiful setting with riverside paths, two venerable arches are rounded and the parapets seem to have been added or replaced since the bridge was first erected, and at a not too recent date either! A stile with gate leads one to a huge shingle beach and upstream the river splashes its way over and in and around the silurian rock which thrusts its way upwards from the river bed at surprising angles. One way traffic over the bridge is the order of the day, but on the south side approach the road is very wide and allows for a lay-by where cars can be parked.

As we make our way back to the town centre we cannot fail to note the beautiful situations in which the various Houses of the School have been placed. Winder House, for example, to the right with playing fields to the east and west of the main road. Soon the sturdy tower of the church of St. Andrew stands out with its unique clock reminding us how quickly time has gone by.

The church has stood in the middle of the town much longer than any other building. It dates from the twelfth century, and even today no small amount of Norman masonry is still to be seen, especially in the north arcade, though much is fifteenth century. However, the doorway within the north porch as well as two buttresses at the west end, and traces of what look like windows in the wall near the tower arch seem to be twelfth century. On entering from the north porch, one immediately realises to one's surprise how spacious the place is. The nave and chancel are continuous and the arcades consist of eight arches on one side and six on the other, all rounded apart from a pointed one at the east end. The east window is a five light affair and depicts the call of St. Andrew. Turning around we see an octagonal font, a splendid example of dedicated workmanship in black marble. Halfway down the nave is a bust of John Dawson, the famous mathematician. A Garsdale boy, he learned a little about medicine, and was intrigued with arithmetic. Having saved £100 by giving what assistance he could to others as a result of his learning, he walked to Edinburgh to learn more about medicine and surgery. Following this he came back to the Sedbergh area until he had saved £300 and then walked to London where he took his diploma. However, he stuck to his mathematics and taught at Sedbergh School – a number of pupils there became Senior Wranglers.

At present the church is in great need of work to keep it in good condition. Routine replacement has revealed hidden problems. A body by the name of Friends of St. Andrew's Church has been formed with a view to raising cash and English Heritage is giving its full support to maintain this wonderful old House of God. Scaffolding will come and go for some time to come. One wonders whether or not the 'flattened' arches of the two most eastward of the north arcade, will be left as they are when further restoration takes place. Another curiosity is in the Lady Chapel. Fairly high up in the corner is a rounded shelf with nothing on it. Did it once have a little statue of Our Lady placed upon it? Maybe, until Henry VIII or even Cromwell thought otherwise.

Apart from the sturdy old four square tower with its eight bells, there are many features outside which attract our attention. Both the north and south porches invite immediate entry, but one must surely pause, especially at the north one, because of the beautiful woodwork of the door. The grotesque heads carved on the dripstones of windows make one wonder what was in the mind of their creator. Another feature on the south wall over an old doorway near the east end of the building is a large sundial resting on two corbels. A great pity some of the carving on it has flaked off. It was given by Braithwaite Otway who died in 1744 and who has a memorial inside. He is remembered for his resistance to the enclosure of commons and was one of the many Otways who lived at Ingmire Hall, just outside the town. Round the church and past the east window to the north-east corner is an extraordinary buttress.

In lighter vein, the following is a note from the Church Wardens' Accounts in A.D.1795:

1*s*. 6*d*. for ale for bell-ringers.
A note was added, signed by the Vicar: "N.B. This will not be allowed in the future".

Sedbergh is not short of a good hostelry or two. The mention of food reminds us of the old tuck shop which stood on or very near the site of the present Post Office. If the school did not have one itself, there was for many years one kept by 'Mother Dilworth'. It was a great treat to go into her old shop. Mrs Dilworth sold all manner of cakes from parkin to jumbles and toffee, all quite small in 'pennorths' and even 'half-pennorths'. A very generous lady – such good value she gave for those well set out goodies. What she might have lost in profit, she made up in turnover. Alas, all good things came to an end when the old lady retired c.1860. We learn that Sedbergh School opened its Grub Shop in 1893.

If we proceed westwards from the Post Office we come to a lane leading up to the Howgills – a massif of hills lumped together, each with rounded or sometimes dome-like summits up to about 2000 feet in height. Outstanding views are obtained in every direction. The hill immediately overlooking Sedbergh is some 1550 feet above sea level and sports the name Winder; a physically fit school boy should be able to climb up to the summit and back to the town which is approximately 550 feet above sea level, in half an hour.

At the east end of the town is the way up the hill to Castlehaw Mound – the site of a motte and bailey. When you visit it, you realise immediately why it was built there as the site commands unrivalled views even though the southern slopes are now well covered with trees and the summit hidden from the main road to Kirkby Stephen. Above the motte and bailey rise the Howgills; ascend Joss Lane or Castlehaw Lane to reach them.

The Kirkby Stephen road takes us to an unusual bridge at an 'S' bend; the bridge itself is situated in the middle of the 'S' and curiously enough is called Straight Bridge. It is a single arched affair and crosses the river Rawthey where it flows through a steep and narrow defile. There is not the slightest suggestion of a hump. Hence the name? Beyond, one is impressed with the delightful area, well wooded and without any intimation of the hard though striking scenery to come. At High Wardses, the energetic can leave their motor car and cross the river to the Cautley Spout, where the water tumbles some several hundred feet in a series of cascades.

Another bridge of two arches crosses the Rawthey much nearer Sedbergh. It is a fine crossing of two rounded arches, regarded by many as lacking in beauty, which leads us to Garsdale, an unusual valley traversed by the river Clough which the road crosses many times. At the first bridge up the valley, we imagine we are 'there', but not quite as there are about another two miles to go. Cross the second bridge and a road sign announces 'Garsdale'. Just around the corner stands the little church of St. John the Baptist with its turret of two bells. Garsdale has no main street as such and one could pass through without realising the existence of a village. Cottages, houses and farms are far from being close together. There is no village inn, but to cater for the modern traveller is a sometimes very welcome filling station.

As we make our way up the valley we think of the days when knitting was an occupation to be reckoned with in Garsdale and Sedbergh as well as Dent. Having reached the road which leads to Garsdale Railway station, we turn down to the Moorcock Inn and make for Wensleydale and Middleham.

MIDDLEHAM

Like so many towns and villages in Wensleydale, Middleham is high and dry above the river Ure, the only major river in Yorkshire named after one of its one-time market towns, Wensley, in this instance.

Middleham's history goes back nearly 2,000 years, for the great Roman Empire left its mark here. Have a look at the unmistakable site east of the castle and cast your mind back to the way of life of the illustrious Roman who lived in the villa which once stood there. Traces of a hypocaust have been found, suggesting under floor heating as well as outer wall panels of hot air. Excavations in the field east of the Sports Field and Pavilion can be approached from the castle or from the little side road on the right a few hundred yards after the last house on the East Witton road. The soil and turf have been replaced, but the unusual and indeed, unnatural ups and downs of the field give one a clue.

First of all, let us enter this unique town with two market places, each with its own cross, on an upward slope from the valley road and absorb that 'something different' atmosphere which it possesses in no small measure. One has the feeling that time has had little effect on the town's character, and even with the coming of modern transport, its appearance has altered very little during the past hundred years. The very stones comprising the buildings have character even though some of them lack beauty. A goodly lot were obviously taken hundreds of years ago from the ruins of the enormous castle which today is well cared for and stands like a guardian overlooking the town.

If the time is appropriate (avoid a public holiday) I advise you to enter one of the several hostelries; the talk varies from horse racing, politics and the weather to sheep farming. If you are lucky, a trainer or stable lad will improve your knowledge of horses, and inform you how horse racing and the love and care of horses 'gets' you. Lambing time varies from February in the valley to early April in the high hills. Such is much of the conversation, and, of course, food and drink to suit all tastes.

The horse racing centres in Yorkshire are in the north, east and south of the county, and here in the heart of Wensleydale, we have great centres for the training of horses and their riders. You have only to go past the top market cross and take the road to Coverdale for a mile or so to see some lovely horses being exercised in the wide open spaces. Sometimes you can see a splendid horse being sedately ridden in the town itself. Horses were first bred and trained in the area by the monks of Jervaulx and Coverham Abbeys for the transport of wool and other commodities, and formed an important part of monastic work. The Dissolution put paid to much of that but few people know that horses have been trained at Middleham for nearly 225 years, and before that and the Dissolution, King Richard III himself had his hunters trained there. There was even a race course at one time. However, Middleham, whilst it has had its dull years

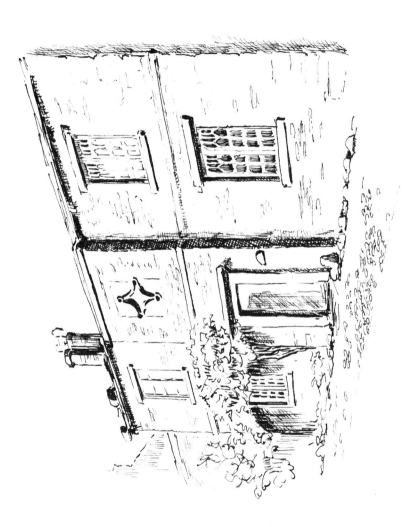

A corner of old Middleham

as a training centre, is on the up turn and has become a force to be reckoned with today.

In 1993, an Open Day was arranged by the Middleham Trainers Association; this was such a success that it was repeated the following year with the result that the Open Day has become an annual event. In addition to the public being able to see something like 400 horses, there are outdoor events where the horses can be seen in action at the 'Gallops' just outside the town. Then there is the Manor House stud which is set in beautiful gardens with views across the valley.

Before exploring the area in and around the castle it is well worthwhile to have a close look at the church of St. Mary and St Alkelda (a Saxon saint), which has served Royalty and the people of Middleham since the thirteenth century. Much of the building, as we see it today, is of a later date. The church was intended to be a collegiate with a Dean and Chapter and eventually became known as The King's College, Middleham under Richard III, but on the latter's death, the title was discarded. However the Dean was licensed to grant probate of wills, and enjoyed power and exemptions granted to the enhanced status of the church. Marriages could take place in the church without a licence or the banns being read prior to the marriage. Shades of Gretna Green! About the time of the Dean's term of office coming to an end and indeed his death in 1754, the practice ceased. Attempts were made to revive the old order, but by the middle of the nineteenth century, Middleham became an ordinary parish church, but what an 'ordinary one'! The Dean and Chapter Stalls in the chancel are each named after Richard III and his wife, Lady Anne Nevill's favourite saints: St. George, St. Ninian, St. Anthony (Rev. Charles Kingsley), one allocated to the Sacristan, a clerk, St. Barbara, St. Cuthbert, St. Catherine and the Dean's Stall, St. Mary. After serving so many years since the fifteenth century, they were replaced by the present ones in the early 1700s. The names of the saints were perpetuated and appear beautifully carved at the head of each stall.

Some 185 years ago, when restoration was taking place, female bones were brought to light and considered to be those of St. Alkelda, who, tradition says, was buried here. The bones were reburied near the lectern. A plate and nearby, Saxon knot-work stone set in the floor indicate this historic spot.

The Lady Chapel with its round arched window and fine glass work, the Richard III window, the font, the north-west aisle window depicting the martyrdom of St. Alkelda, are all 'musts' for the visitor. Standing near the font is a large tomb cover of one Robert Thornton, the 23rd. Abbot of Jervaulx who died in 1533. It is thought to have been brought to Middleham for protection at the time of the Dissolution. Around the borders of the stone are the words:

ORATE PRO A'I'A DOMINI ROBERTI THORNTON ABBAT HUI DOMI
JERVALLIS VICIMI SC'DI

The aptness of the carved work in the central part of the stone is very worthy of note.

Upper Market Cross, Middleham

A gold double sided locket in wonderful condition was found as recently as 1985 in a field close to the castle and is known as the Middleham Jewel. An exact replica is to be seen in a glass case on the west wall of the church; a switch lights up the jewel for a short time and automatically switches itself off. The replica was given by Mrs Lenore Peacock of Middleham Manor, in whose field 10 inches below ground the jewel was found, and is in memory of her family. The detail on the jewel is remarkable and a wonderful example of medieval goldsmith's art. The original is now in the Yorkshire Museum.

To the west of the church beyond the churchyard are the remains of St. Alkelda's well; its waters were said to have curative properties. Due to house building nearby, the natural drainage has been disturbed and the well is dry.

And now for the enormous castle, carefully kept in trim since 1984 by English Heritage. Entering by means of a wooden bridge over the surrounding ditch (formerly by means of a drawbridge) one passes through a gracious archway into the castle where some 500 years ago, the Duke of Gloucester, later Richard III spent some years as a young man. The Earl of Warwick, the King Maker, owned the place as well as Raby and Brancpeth in County Durham; on his death, Edward IV gave it to Richard who was crowned in 1483. The latter made Middleham his principal castle in the north of England, often stated to be the Windsor of the North; also claiming this distinction is little Cawood on the Ouse south of York, and not without reason!

To obtain a bird's eye view of the lay-out, one must climb the restored staircase of the keep which leads to a platform. Apart from the wonderful view, especially on a clear day, of the surrounding country including Castle Bolton built by the Scropes, there is a first rate view of the Motte and Bailey built by the Normans. The latter lies on what is known as William's Hill, and the breathless climb southwards rewards one amply. Today, of course, there are only the remains of the one-time stronghold. The size is far greater than one would imagine when seen from the castle, and the views are even better than those obtained from the viewing platform of the latter.

A striking feature of the castle must be the great height of nearly all the stonework considering that it fell into disuse so many years ago. It was not so much a fortified stronghold as a royal residence with a vast estate around it where royalty and lords and ladies of the highest rank were lavishly entertained. Although it had its moments during the Civil War, and a number of Parliamentary prisoners were kept there, it gradually fell into disuse, except perhaps part of it was used as an estate office and staff lodgings. At the end of the nineteenth century, it was bought by Samuel Cunliffe Lister of Bradford Manningham Mills fame. He became the first Lord Masham, and his son the Second Lord did some urgent repairs – you will see several lintels of doorways marked 'M' alone and some with an 'M' and a date.

As we make our way into the town itself, we cannot fail to notice the unusual market cross with two interesting items of stonework built on top of the steps. One is like a chalice and the other is a time weathered stone model of a boar. A plaque on the south side reads:

THIS CROSS IS THOUGHT TO COMMEMORATE THE GRANT OB-
TAINED FOR MIDDLEHAM IN 1479 OF A FAIR AND MARKET
TWICE YEARLY IN WHITSUN WEEK AND AT THE FEAST OF ST.
SIMON AND ST. JUDE BY RICHARD DUKE OF GLOUCESTER,
LATER KING RICHARD III. THE HERALDIC ANIMAL MAY BE HIS
OWN COGNISANCE OF THE WHITE BOAR, OR THE EMBLEM OF
THE FAMILY OF HIS WIFE ANNE NEVILL CO-HEIRESS OF THE
LORDSHIP OF MIDDLEHAM

Look closely at the stonework to see the connections.

Going down the main street, we come to the other market place with its own cross and a steep hill on the left. Descending, we find many quaint buildings on both sides, but one on the left is particularly attractive – it is called 'Brief Cottage'. Just below, on the same side is the main entrance to the church, up a side street, if you please! Incidentally, there is also the entrance to no mean sets of racing stables.

And so we leave Middleham with reluctance, albeit with a great deal of thought, knowing full well that there must be much more to see.

N